MW01529093

A scene from the Second Stage Theatre production of "Sympathetic Magic." Set design

SYMPATHETIC MAGIC

BY
LANFORD WILSON

★

★

DRAMATISTS
PLAY SERVICE
INC.

SYMPATHETIC MAGIC
Copyright © 1998, Lanford Wilson

All Rights Reserved

CAUTION: Professionals and amateurs are hereby warned that performance of SYMPATHETIC MAGIC is subject to payment of a royalty. It is fully protected under the copyright laws of the United States of America, and of all countries covered by the International Copyright Union (including the Dominion of Canada and the rest of the British Commonwealth), and of all countries covered by the Pan-American Copyright Convention, the Universal Copyright Convention, the Berne Convention, and of all countries with which the United States has reciprocal copyright relations. All rights, including professional/amateur stage rights, motion picture, recitation, lecturing, public reading, radio broadcasting, television, video or sound recording, all other forms of mechanical or electronic reproduction, such as CD-ROM, CD-I, DVD, information storage and retrieval systems and photocopying, and the rights of translation into foreign languages, are strictly reserved. Particular emphasis is placed upon the matter of readings, permission for which must be secured from the Author's agent in writing.

The English language stock and amateur stage performance rights in the United States, its territories, possessions and Canada for SYMPATHETIC MAGIC are controlled exclusively by DRAMATISTS PLAY SERVICE, INC., 440 Park Avenue South, New York, NY 10016. No professional or nonprofessional performance of the Play may be given without obtaining in advance the written permission of DRAMATISTS PLAY SERVICE, INC., and paying the requisite fee.

Inquiries concerning all other rights should be addressed to International Creative Management, Inc., 40 West 57th Street, New York, NY 10019. Attn: Mitch Douglas.

SPECIAL NOTE
Anyone receiving permission to produce SYMPATHETIC MAGIC is required to give credit to the Author as sole and exclusive Author of the Play on the title page of all programs distributed in connection with performances of the Play and in all instances in which the title of the Play appears for purposes of advertising, publicizing or otherwise exploiting the Play and/or a production thereof. The name of the Author must appear on a separate line, in which no other name appears, immediately beneath the title and in size of type equal to 50% of the size of the largest, most prominent letter used for the title of the Play. No person, firm or entity may receive credit larger or more prominent than that accorded the Author. The following acknowledgment must appear on the title page in all programs distributed in connection with performances of the Play:

World premiere production by Second Stage Theatre, April 16, 1997
Artistic Director   Producing Director
Carole Rothman   Suzanne Schwartz Davidson
with a grant from the Lila Wallace-Reader's Digest Fund

SPECIAL NOTE ON SONGS AND RECORDINGS
For performances of copyrighted songs, arrangements or recordings mentioned in this Play, the permission of the copyright owner(s) must be obtained. Other songs, arrangements or recordings may be substituted provided permission from the copyright owner(s) of such songs, arrangements or recordings is obtained; or songs, arrangements or recordings in the public domain may be substituted.

2

ACKNOWLEDGMENT

To the Second Stage Theatre who commissioned this play with funds from the Lila Wallace-Reader's Digest Fund Resident Theatre Initiative; the Harold and Mimi Steinberg Charitable Trust; the Educational Foundation of America and Chase Manhattan Bank. Second Stage Artistic Director Carole Rothman, Producing Director Suzanne Schwartz Davidson and especially Literary Director, Chris Burney.

To the many friends who read one or two of the endless drafts of this play over the fifteen years of its composition and encouraged me to hang tough and finish the thing. Primarily, or most insistently: David Kahn, Timothy Mason, Claris Nelson, Bobby Cannivale, Kevin Corstange, Michael Powell, Florence Fink, Tanya Berezin, John Hawkins, Bill Hoffman, Bill Leavengood, Michael Respolli, Marshall Mason and Christopher Reeve for whom I wrote the part of Don.

My sincere thanks and profound gratitude to Dr. Ata Sarajedini, Associate at Kitt Peak National Observatory, for guiding me through the observatory and putting up with endless questions over the following many months; to Dr. Joan Koss, Department of Anthropology and Dr. David Burstein, Department of Physics and Astronomy at Arizona State University; and to my associate, Allison Dillon, for finding them.

Their suggestions, guidance, assistance and patience were invaluable in allowing me to tell this story. And a warm appreciative nod to John Simon, Michael Feingold and Clive Barnes who understood it.

SYMPATHETIC MAGIC was produced by Second Stage Theatre (Carole Rothman, Artistic Director; Suzanne Schwartz Davidson, Producing Director) in New York City on March 18, 1997. It was directed by Marshall W. Mason; the set design was by John Lee Beatty; the costume design was by Laura Crow; the lighting design was by Dennis Parichy; the sound design was by Chuck London; the fight staging was by B. H. Barry; the production stage manager was Denise Yaney; and the stage manager was Karen Potosnak. The cast was as follows:

IAN ANDERSON ....David Bishins
DON WALKER ....Jeff McCarthy
BARBARA DE BIERS..Ellen Lancaster
CARL CONKLIN WHITE ....Herb Foster
PAULY SCOTT..David Pittu
SUSAN OLMSTED ....Dana Millican
LIZ BARNARD ....Tanya Berezin
MICKEY PICCO ....Jordan Mott

CHARACTERS

IAN ANDERSON (ANDY) — An astrophysicist, 30ish.

DON WALKER — An Episcopalian priest, 35.

BARBARA DE BIERS — A sculptor, 30s; Don's half-sister.

PAULY SCOTT — A Chorus master, soon 30.

SUE OLMSTEAD — Liz's assistant, 24 or so, on leave from law school.

MICKEY PICCO — Andy's co-worker, 30. A post doc.

LIZ BARNARD — Barbara and Don's mother, a retired anthropologist, late 50s.

CARL CONKLIN WHITE — 60s, head of Andy's department.

SETTING

Places are indicated and sometimes described. What I really want is just the barest indication of the various locations in and around San Francisco. A unit set. One scene should flow into the next instantaneously, overlapping fluidly. Let the lights tell us where we are and when.

SYMPATHETIC MAGIC

ACT ONE

The house lights are on.

The stage is set for a slide lecture: a screen, and to one side, a speaker's dais.

Andy comes to the podium, coughing, clearing his throat. He is in his thirties, good looking, brilliant, charming and knows it.

ANDY.   Oh, dear god. 9 A.M. is brutal on an astronomer. We're a nocturnal breed. *(Looking out to the audience.)*
Okay. Realize you're getting a percentage of me here — I'm much better across the table, at a decent hour, over a beer. My name is Ian Anderson. They call me Andy because I've always hated the name Ian. My middle name is Welsh, unpronounceable, embarrassing, and you'll never know it.
When I was at the University of Chicago, we used to go to Second City, a comedy club there. They sell tapes from the club's early heydays, and probably their maddest star was Severen Darden. Of course, my favorite of Darden's routines is announced by: "And now, ladies and gentlemen, Professor Valter Vandervogelvider will present a short talk on the Universe." And Darden begins: *(Falling into a slight German accent.)*
"Now, why — you will ask me — have I chosen to speak on the universe, rather than some other topic.... Well, it's very simple. There isn't anything else." *(Beat.)*
So I don't call these lectures "A Short Talk on The Universe." Even the *known* universe — I've always loved that expression — is largely unknown to us. Astronomers don't call it the known universe, I don't know where that expression came from. We might say the "visible" universe. *(Musing.)*

7

The visible universe. I have a demonstration here. As you may know one theory is that space is curved, it bends, almost doubles back on itself, rather like an English saddle, so this isn't quite accurate, but — I'm going to ask you to look around you, up and down and around this room, wall to wall, floor to ceiling. The *volume* of this room. And assume this room to be the universe. This is a demonstration of scale. I always loved those in school. *(He takes a folded sheet of paper from his inside jacket pocket and begins to unfold it.)*

Just to show you how conscientious I am, we live in a great old warehouse at the edge of the golf course, that practically overhangs the ocean. I walked the hundred yards or so down to the beach this morning, right to the edge of the water and picked up a grain of sand. Still wet. It would taste of salt. So this is a *completely authentic* grain of sand. So. Assume the volume of this room to be the vastness of the universe. This grain of sand, then, represents — with all our instruments — what we can *see* of it. The visible universe. *(Beat.)*

In other words we're legally blind. There's the small matter that: There is some contention about the size of the universe; and the not insignificant matter of the "dark matter," that seems to make up about 98 percent of the mass of the universe, and which we can't see at all. And dust and litter and the speed of light and — The presumption of postulating any sort of picture, let alone history, from so inferior a sampling is pretty staggering.

But, of course, we haven't let that stop us for a moment.

We're going to be looking at a number of slides this morning talking about galaxy clusters and super cluster complexes and why they cluster, and that dark mysterious matter, that we can't see, called dark matter — and what it may have to do with all this clustering and chaos. *(He steps aside, looking at the screen, then to where there might be a stage manager, above and behind the audience.)*

If we could kill the lights, please. *(Waits a moment.)*

If we could — *(Total blackout. Of both the audience and stage.)*

Thank you. *(Lights come up almost immediately [the screen is gone] on the very dim interior of a moderately prosperous Episcopalian*

8

Church. The altar is U. The church is closed, the only light comes from the windows on an overcast day. A priest unlocks a side door and lets himself in, walks across the church, genuflects perfunctually, goes to the far door and stops. This is Father Donald Walker, maybe 35, tall, handsome, and rather remote. He senses someone in the church. He looks out.)

DON. I'm sorry, the church is closed.

BARBARA. The side door was open.

DON. Can I help you?

BARBARA. You say that better than you used to. It sounds like you really mean it now. Your pews and benches are just hard wood? You don't have cushions for your parishioners to kneel on?

DON. It keeps them humble. *(He has recognized her and walks toward her. Barbara is a strong, straightforward, attractive woman in her 30s. She wears a trench coat over jeans.)*

BARBARA. *(Looking up, we can't see at what.)* I was looking at the banner. Is that Greek?

DON. Hebrew.

BARBARA. What does it say?

DON. "Yahweh."

BARBARA. And that means...?

DON. "I ... AM."

BARBARA. Whoa.... And you're not.

DON. Something like that.

BARBARA. Are we high, low, or middle Episcopalian?

DON. Maybe upper middle. What brings you up here?

BARBARA. I was driving. I ended up here.

DON. Did you want to talk about something?

BARBARA. I think I'm talked out right now. Or thought out. How are you?

DON. I'm fine. You don't look too great.

BARBARA. Thanks.

DON. Are you taking care of yourself?

BARBARA. I had my hair done yesterday, first time in a year. I got a manicure, a facial. This is as good as it gets.

DON. Why are you thought out? What have you been thinking?

9

BARBARA. You mean you haven't been following my meteoric decline? Everyone thinks he knows what I've been thinking. You can read it in all the papers in the Bay Area.

DON. Is that bad?

BARBARA. Don. They sound like I'm advocating public castration of every male on the planet.

DON. I thought you were.

BARBARA. After those reviews, maybe a few. Some bastard in the *Chronicle* said one piece was five railroad ties bolted together to look like a pair of goats fornicating in great agony.

DON. And that wasn't your intention.

BARBARA. I thought it was a very compelling arrangement of…. *(Waves it off, laughing.)* All I can see now is….

DON. — Goats fornicating in great agony.

BARBARA. No, the pieces look good in the space. Not last night, with two hundred people sloshing white zinfandel all over the gallery.

DON. Your opening was last night.

BARBARA. I wouldn't have known if you showed or not; I was there half an hour.

DON. Is this a crisis of faith? You're being badly received and it's all ashes ashes ashes?

BARBARA. I think you have to be a great success before you discover it's not been worth it.

DON. You still living with — the scientist?

BARBARA. Ian. Anderson. Andy. Astrophysicist. We've still got the warehouse. I thought you were going to ask if I was still living in sin.

DON. That would be for you to say.

BARBARA. Then I imagine I am.

DON. It seems like a good arrangement.

BARBARA. Yeah, everyone's crazy about Andy. *(Beat.)* How's mom?

DON. We have to realize mom may not get any better.

BARBARA. We can hope she doesn't get any worse.

DON. *(After a second he lets it pass.)* Even sick she doesn't show it. Her eyes are going. She blames her glasses. I'm glad she kept the apartment all these years.

BARBARA. It's still very weird having her back here.

DON. I keep thinking we should all act like a family now.

BARBARA. Ha! How does a family act?

DON. She's trying to get used to dictating. You know she's writing a memoir.

BARBARA. Yeah, well, I always wondered what her side of the story would sound like.

DON. She'll come out smelling like a rose.

BARBARA. You can lay money on that. She was supposed to be there last night. She doesn't know what to do with me. You were the one she liked.

DON. I know, it was embarrassing. You'd leave the room she'd grab my hand and say, "You're the one I love the most."

BARBARA. I think I have her to thank for being an artist. She was always running off to hell or wherever — Zaire — with you. I coveted that time so much — my room was a jungle — literally, a jungle — that I'd made out of cardboard and rope.... Green painted palm trees and ... I'd come to these impossibly deep gorges with you and her and an entourage of bearers, crossing the Niger on swinging bridges of something like spider webs and vines. Knives and guns stuck in my belt. Saving you and mom from some horrible disaster. That's what comes from having no one to play with.

DON. I don't think I'm so much her favorite anymore. Maybe I've disappointed her.

BARBARA. I always thought she was glad you didn't marry so she wouldn't have to share you.

DON. I know.

BARBARA. She just liked your dad better than mine.

DON. Who wouldn't?

BARBARA. You've got that right. (*A hallway at the college. Andy walks from the lecture room, Carl calls to him. Carl is older, the head of Andy's department. There is the usual rivalry.*)

CARL. Andy. A moment.

ANDY. Carl, hi. Where the hell did you jump out from — ?

CARL. — We're going to have to talk.

ANDY. Talk? Uh ... fine. About anything in particular?

CARL. How does Wednesday look to you?

11

ANDY.   Wednesday looks like I'm going to wish I was dead. I have the lecture again Tuesday morning at nine, classes all day and our first observation run all night.

CARL.   — I am familiar with the schedule of my department. I'm sure you'll be as fresh as butter.

ANDY.   I can't give you any guarantee —

CARL.   *(Abrupt.)* It looks like tomorrow night's going to be a washout.

ANDY.   Mickey and I are hoping they'll be wrong about the rain.

CARL.   I have a rather full plate. Why don't you drop by for breakfast?

ANDY.   I don't believe it, Carl, you actually made a joke. Oh, I'm sorry, you didn't realize that was funny. I don't eat breakfast.

CARL.   Most important meal of the day. *(Carl turns and leaves, Andy exits the other way. Pauly enters the church. He crosses toward the other door. Pauly has stopped, realizing someone is in the church. Pauly is a gay Choir Master and a fine man. He will soon be 30 and might be called cute. He comes toward Barbara and Don, squinting myopically.)*

PAULY.   You're early, that's unforgivable. The church is supposed to be closed till…. Don? What are you doing sitting in the total…? Oh, sorry, I didn't realize you were with —— Barbara? Oh, my god! Girl!

BARBARA.   Hello, Pauly.

PAULY.   What a treat!

BARBARA.   It's great to see you.

PAULY.   I saw your show.

BARBARA.   Oh, please.

PAULY.   It blew my doors off. I was totally prepared and it still killed me. I stayed for two hours. I was shaking all over and bawling, but I do that. You do know it's brilliant. I mean I worry about that. That the artist doesn't know she's reaching people.

BARBARA.   What are you doing here in the middle —

PAULY.   — Don't interrupt me, I'm not finished gushing. Does it bother you to have people fawn and slaver all over you

12

and tell you it really is the strongest, bravest work I've seen in years?

BARBARA.   In confidence? I can take it. What are you doing here in the middle of the day?

PAULY.   Choir practice. Not the real choir, I've got a new ad hoc group. We're singing —— well, I wouldn't call it singing. They rather redefine the concept of pitch.

BARBARA.   What happened to your regular choir? I love them.

PAULY.   Aren't they? No, they're still going — ack! I started to say *strong*. No, this is a bunch of music lovers and lovers of music lovers who love to sing and never have and they're loving it and I'm going crazy. We're calling them the Town Choir. They're a great group, a sort of thrown together kind of —

DON.   — People with AIDS.

PAULY.   Thanks. Trust Don for the bottom line. And their friends and wives and husbands. A *lot* of women.

BARBARA.   Oh, god.

PAULY.   Only we're not calling them the AIDS Chorale for exactly the reason of that kind of overwhelmingly warm reception.

DON.   And his gay friends tell us AIDS is no longer a sexy issue.

PAULY.   They're *my* gay friends now, you notice.

BARBARA.   No, I think it's great.

PAULY.   Please. In a minute you forget they're sick, and just want to knock them all senseless. Almost none of them reads music, so of course we're doing Mozart! It's a totally new experience for me, which is what we're here for, right? How *are* you? I thought you'd be there last night.

BARBARA.   I left early.

PAULY.   *(He starts to get up, sits back down.)* You should have stayed to see every artist in the Bay Area get roaring drunk on jealousy and free booze. Oh, god. I can't believe I'm actually sitting down for five minutes.

BARBARA.   You look thin.

DON.   He's doing too much, as usual.

PAULY.   I know I look like shit.

BARBARA. You're always gorgeous.

PAULY. There's just so much to do and this goddamned disease just swept my choir, half of it, *away.* Just devastated it, one by one by ... I never knew who was going to show. I'm not talking the new group, I'm talking about trying to rebuild the finest church choir in — at least California.

BARBARA. I know.

PAULY. Oh, don't listen to me. I'm just bone-achingly tired. From work, nothing's *wrong* with me, I'm perfectly healthy as hell. I haven't had sex of any kind in two years. I'm being very good so I can go to heaven and just fucking punch God's lights out for this. I'm not joking.

DON. Pauly, we don't need that.

PAULY. Oh, kiss my ass, Father. I am so much healthier just being Don's co-worker. It was very disconcerting in public to have to call your lover "Father." Did he tell you he's going straight?

DON. I didn't say that.

BARBARA. Not in so many words.

PAULY. *(Getting up.)* He never speaks in so many words. And! Speaking of my ass, I've got to get off it and run through the music. I'm so glad I got to see you. My gang is going to be traipsing in here before long, though....

BARBARA. I know, I'll get out.

PAULY. I'd say stay, but not yet. Give me a week. *(To Don.)* You're going to drop by at some point? As a surprise? *(Back to Barbara.)* They love it. They're all totally in love with him. I could tell them about that. *(Going.)* It's the only reason they show up. I'm leaving this door open now.

DON. Fine.

PAULY. *(To Barbara.)* Love you, keep working, honey, it's all we've got.

BARBARA. Tell me about it. *(Pauly is gone.)* Do the Episcopalians have saints?

DON. Everyone doesn't respond to him the way you do. *(Andy and Barbara's place. Barbara's studio, an old warehouse. Huge doors open to the sky, we hear the ocean. Barbara takes off her coat; she's in jeans and a dirty tank top. Andy bursts in, ripping off his tie, jacket*

14

and shirt and kicking off his shoes.)

ANDY. I am totally fucking wiped out. Some guy comes up after the lecture, and without even saying I had been interesting, Carl standing right there, this guy says, "Doctor Anderson, how do you reconcile that with Christian Theology and the Son of Man?" And instead of saying, "I don't, you pagan asshole," I stood there with my thumb up my —— saying, "That's a very good question."

BARBARA. "I should address that in a future lecture."

ANDY. Buy another ticket. Hustling my act. *(Taking her in his arms, kissing her.)* Oh, god. How can you look so dirty and smell so clean?

BARBARA. Alchemy. *(Touching his chin.)* I think I'm going to need that chin for a piece I'm working on.

ANDY. A representation of the chin, right, not the chin itself.

BARBARA. What did Carl want?

ANDY. *(He continues taking off his clothes, down to his shorts.)* I spent the entire lecture bitching the hour, saying I'm grotesque before 5 in the evening, the bastard hears every word and asks me to come by for breakfast. Which the entire school knows he has at 6 A.M. On his terrace. In his fucking dressing gown. On top of that, it's supposed to rain tomorrow night. We'll end up canceling the run sure as hell. Come down to the beach with me.

BARBARA. Two things: you've got to go see Mickey.

ANDY. I have to call him, he's probably been watching the Weather Channel all day.

BARBARA. Benji left him.

ANDY. Oooh ... god! For real?

BARBARA. Well, she took all the furniture.

ANDY. Oh ... Christ. He's going to be crying. I can't stand Mickey crying. Benji was no good for him anyway.

BARBARA. I could care less about a girl who allows herself to be called by a dog's name. The other thing — if you've ever had doubts about your fertility or mine, I have reassuring news for you.

ANDY. "If I've ever had doubts about my fertility...." Are you — what? — you're overdue?

15

BARBARA. I think you could say that I'm overdue.

ANDY. How much?

BARBARA. If I were an airplane, they'd have called off the search.

ANDY. That's astonishing.

BARBARA. Apparently the rabbit committed suicide as I came in the door. You wouldn't be grinning if you were the one retaining forty gallons of water every morning.

ANDY. Are you sure?

BARBARA. Totally.

ANDY. Woa! *(Sits.)* Let me get my mind around this.

BARBARA. Anyway, I went over to the clinic and they —

ANDY. — What clinic?

BARBARA. Andy, for one minute come on down from the stars.

ANDY. Oh. Sure. Okay, I'm with you. You went over to the clinic.

BARBARA. They can't take me till Friday morning, so I've got four more days of this.

ANDY. What am I doing on Friday?

BARBARA. You don't need to come.

ANDY. I can get someone to cover my classes.

BARBARA. Totally unnecessary. But don't forget we've got Pauly's birthday party Friday night.

ANDY. Good excuse to miss that. You OK?

BARBARA. I will be. It's amazing what goes on physically. The whole body is on Red Alert. It's no fun.

ANDY. You've been wearing the thing?

BARBARA. The diaphragm, the jelly, the douche, the pill.

ANDY. Jesus. Can we sue? The little buggers got through all that, huh?

BARBARA. Combat-ready little suckers, huh?

ANDY. That's fantastic.

BARBARA. Oh, shut up.

ANDY. No, that gets a guy pumped-up. It's biological. I mean, for you it may be about making love, caresses, tenderness, for a guy, basically it's about ejaculation. Breeding. That's what we're there for. Here I am, I'm your man.

16

BARBARA. I'm hip.

ANDY. Plant that seed. Get a crop started here.

BARBARA. That is very gross.

ANDY. Well, I'm sorry, we can't do a thing about it. It's chemistry. All this brain work is just to sort of hose us down.

BARBARA. I hate to disillusion you but women have the same chemical reactions. What do you think "getting hot" means?

ANDY. That's just your body telling you — hey, this guy is good breeding stock here.

BARBARA. Oh, stop.

ANDY. To my knowledge I've never had sex with a pregnant woman.

BARBARA. Totally redundant experience. And I've never been less interested. Which is probably part of the package.

ANDY. *(Musing.)* "If you've ever had doubts about your fertility, I have reassuring news for you." It's hardly "I bring you good tidings of great joy which shall be to all people." *(He leaves the room and will return in a moment putting on swimming trunks, carrying a towel.)*

BARBARA. You got that right.

ANDY. Maybe we should think about this a minute.

BARBARA. About what? Oh, go away.

ANDY. I mean, right now you think it'd probably interfere with your work. But — and your philosophy and your head.

BARBARA. And your work and your head.

ANDY. And my work.

BARBARA. And neither of us would make particularly good parents....

ANDY. Horrible parents. And, thanks to your bitch of a mother, you had a rotten childhood....

BARBARA. That about covers it, don't you think? I work. That's all I claim to be about. Go on down to the beach. *(Barbara exits, Andy stays a moment. Don and Sue enter the church garden, San Francisco. They each have a glass of red wine. Sue is 24 or so, very pretty, intelligent and impressionable.)*

DON. The church was built in 1837, remodeled in the 1850s after the gold rush. The chapel was added at the turn of the century along with a lot of remodeling, wiring, some of the plumbing. So it's essentially a collage of fragments.

ANDY. *(Calls off to Barbara.)* When is the sex of a fetus determined? Almost instantaneously, isn't it?

SUE. I love the courtyard the buildings make.

BARBARA. *(Off.)* Go on down to the beach.

ANDY. So it's a boy or a girl already. *(There is no reply to Andy. After a while he will grab the towel and go out the huge door, heading for the ocean.)*

DON. I know, the church, the school, the rectory and the old bus barn, which may yet have a new life. Where's Pauly?

SUE. Giving notes to the choir.

DON. That may take a while. You're picking up mom?

SUE. Yeah. Driving down to Barbara's place.

DON. You liking San Francisco?

SUE. I love it.

DON. "Sue." That's a good name.

SUE. I know: good name for a lawyer. It's a clue in all the crossword puzzles.

DON. That's right. Mom said you're a lawyer. Do you —

SUE. No! Lord! I was in law school. Plus working like a dope as a paralegal drudge. I'm glad to be shut of it.

DON. Research stuff, that sort of thing?

SUE. Precedents, writing most of their briefs. *Typing* for godsake. Sorry Father. *(Don waves off the fact she's taken the Lord's name in vain; don't be silly.)*

DON. Don, please.

SUE. Thank you. I'm just grateful I learned word processing, working with an Olympus unit. Your mom has an incredible mind.

DON. How's the book coming?

SUE. Oh, she's a hoot. She's slashing out at everybody. I think her frustration with having to dictate everything on a microcassette makes her pretty choleric.

DON. No, she was always the rebel anthropologist. *Time* magazine called her Anthropology's Only Angry Young Man. I was hoping writing a book would keep her off the street.

SUE. Afraid not. Half the day with the street gangs, half dictating. You're in it.

18

DON. I'm in the book? She's writing about the family? I mean her marriages and divorces, lovers, all the moves and fights and scandals and recriminations?

SUE. I'm typing like a madwoman, but I'm gasping. She'll casually drop something like, "It was raining. We were drinking snake's blood. They had just sacrificed a *kid.*" Even after I realize that a "kid" is probably only a young goat. I mean, snake's blood!?

DON. How am I in it?

SUE. When you guys were in Africa. The Shaman and the women there. That's what I mean, it's memoir but it's anthropology and sociology and medicine and magic. It's amazing.

DON. You're not drinking your wine.

SUE. It's a little early for me. Catch me later in the day I'll drink you under the table.

DON. How am I in it?

SUE. When you had the fever; the witch-doctor who took you away and buried you in mud. She said you had a temperature of a hundred four three nights running. Imagine a mother trusting them.

DON. Not your ordinary mother. The drugs were having no effect, the quinine; I'm allergic to anything else.

SUE. And you haven't been ill since. Not a day.

DON. Nope.

SUE. *I want that mud.* How old were you?

DON. I was out of it with the fever. I was six. That's what you meant by I'm in it?

SUE. You're really worried aren't you? That's all so far. I'm hoping for more. *(Barbara slides open the door of the warehouse. Sue joins Barbara and her mother. Liz is in her late fifties and is imposing. Very straight-arrow, cunning, all business.)*

BARBARA. All the buildings along this road back onto the golf course.

SUE. It's incredible.

BARBARA. When we throw open both doors we have the golf course on one side and the ocean on the other. The occasional errant golf ball or burned-out caddie, gaping at me trying to work. One said, what are you building? I said an airplane, he thought that was cool.

LIZ.   How can you afford this?

BARBARA.   Thanks, mom, we like it too. Actually it's pretty reasonable, the Club just left it standing because they thought it was picturesque. The kitchen is through here, dining — bedrooms upstairs. I'm not into "showing the house."

LIZ.   We'll assume the usual amenities.

BARBARA.   I'm afraid it's not Africa. We have indoor plumbing; beds, pillows, sheets.

LIZ.   You'll have to cope somehow.

SUE.   How did she go into those villages? Most of them'd never seen a white woman. Weren't you afraid they'd rape you or have you for lunch? Women must have hated you.

LIZ.   They usually pitied me. Wanted to rub mud in my hair.

SUE.   I just pick up the tapes and take them home. I never get to grill her.

LIZ.   It was just: Where do you get your water; what do you eat; is it safe to lie down here? You should travel more. The world is decorous and civilized. Those are not qualities I particularly admire, you understand.

BARBARA.   I'd be more comfortable with you in Africa than down in the ghettos.

LIZ.   Not that different, sugar. It's all tribal. Behaviorily East Oakland's not that different from Wall Street.

BARBARA.   How the hell did a white woman ever get to a black street gang?

LIZ.   The local preacher, one social worker they almost trust, and Africa, honey. I know more about colors, gangs, than they do. And African history, oppression. Jungle warfare.

BARBARA.   She'll be teaching them to make blow-guns.

SUE.   *(To Barbara.)* Oh, I went to your opening with Pauly. I loved it. I mean, you know, he sort of hogs the whole experience, carrying on and crying, it's not easy to know what your own feelings are.

BARBARA.   I know what you mean.

SUE.   I know that doesn't mean anything to you, what someone else thinks about your work.

BARBARA.   Where did you get that?

SUE. I thought artists were indifferent to all that.

BARBARA. Let me tell you about the fine line between indifference and masochism.

LIZ. I hope to god you're not listening to those anxious sycophants — every asshole has an opinion. You've got such muscle and power, being a woman, you terrify the shit out of them. If you were a man they'd be on their knees fellating you in Union Square. Your work was always too powerful for some people to take.

BARBARA. Dubious distinction, believe me.

SUE. I'd hate that, criticism and all. I guess if you decide to be an artist it comes with the territory.

LIZ. You don't decide to be an artist. I knew you were an artist by the time you were five. God knows where you get it, I claim no credit.

BARBARA. Dad was always so morose and self-pitying, I had to do something to get away.

LIZ. Ha! So did I. *(An outside cafe. Sue joins Pauly.)*

PAULY. Hold it a second, I see someone I know. *(Calling.)* Andy! You'll love this guy.

SUE. It's Barbara's guy, I know him.

PAULY. Of course you do. He would make it a point. *(Andy joins them, looking a little hurried, but pleased to see friends.)*

ANDY. Hi, Pauly. "Sue," isn't it? I didn't know you guys knew each other.

PAULY. Years and years.

SUE. Pauly got me the job with Liz. I'm forever in his debt.

PAULY. We were in school together. Sit.

ANDY. You went to Stanford?

SUE. Lane and Snider.

PAULY. High school and Junior High.

SUE. Fort Wayne, Indiana.

PAULY. I was a senior, Susan was in seventh grade. We lived across the street from each other. Walked to school together. Holding hands. Deeply in love.

SUE. Then Pauly met the guard on the basketball team.

PAULY. I would have said that. *(To Andy.)* What's with you?

ANDY. Did you happen to notice those black clouds on the

horizon? We're supposed to be at the observatory tonight. First night of only three.

SUE.   Unlikely. What are you doing? At the observatory. What's your project?

ANDY.   Oh, god. First, we're testing a lot of new, very sophisticated equipment: microscopic "lenslets," a new photo detector, computerized sensors, that in theory will boost the power of our lowly old telescope here to close to the power of the Keck Observatory in Hawaii.

PAULY.   Really? That's phenomenal. *(To Sue.)* Keck is probably the biggest —

ANDY.   — Best ground-based telescope in the world. Which would make our telescope damn important. Then, secondly, if all the new stuff works, we'll be looking at a number of very distant objects that might be galaxies in the process of forming. And if they are galaxies we'll try to determine if their centers contain a black hole. Mickey and I will be testing the new equipment here and we have a guy on the big telescope in Hawaii. Only he's just making the observations and F. T. P'ing them to us. We'll analyze the data here.

SUE.   He's "Peeing" you the observations?

ANDY.   Sorry. F. T. P. File Transfer Protocol.

PAULY.   Scientific "e" mail.

ANDY.   If we wash out here we can look at what's coming in from Hawaii. So, we'll be looking at the farthest and oldest object yet seen from earth.

PAULY.   So you'll go up to the observatory either way.

ANDY.   If it rains I can have the data transferred to the computer in my office.

SUE.   When did you get interested in astronomy?

ANDY.   That's like me asking you, when did you decide to be a woman?

SUE.   I'm not sure I have

ANDY.   When I was a kid. As soon as I could formulate any thought about what I wanted to know, I wanted to know it all. How it all works, where it began, where it ends. It's the only question.

SUE.   What if you find the answer?

ANDY. Then we'll know.

SUE. Then what's left to work on?

PAULY. Human behavior, chaos, viruses, feeding the masses.

ANDY. I can't imagine how anyone could think about doing anything else. Don't even think about challenging it.

SUE. *(Actually quite taken with Andy.)* I hadn't thought about challenging it.

ANDY. I didn't mean you. I just meant, anyone. Or ... we don't have to get into it right now. Come see my lecture tomorrow. I could use the inspiration.

SUE. Aren't you living with my boss' daughter?

ANDY. Oh, no, I didn't mean it like that, I.... *(They are all standing to leave.)*

SUE. Yeah, sure.

ANDY. Just come see my —

SUE. No, I'd like to. I will.

PAULY. What I'd like to see is an observatory run.

SUE. That would be cool.

ANDY. They have an observatory at Stanford.

PAULY. I took physics — I never made it up there.

ANDY. Come on up — we'll welcome the distraction. Not tonight, it looks like we won't be there.

SUE. I'd love it.

PAULY. Great.

ANDY. That doesn't get you off the hook, coming to the lecture. I like to have someone I know in the audience.

PAULY. Straight men are all a pack of brazen whores. Come up and see my etchings. I'm out of here. *(Liz stops Pauly before he can leave, the others go separate ways.)*

LIZ. Pauly. I'm seeing something very alarming among your people.

PAULY. Among my people?

LIZ. I'm talking about unsafe sex. I'm finding an alarming apathy, in San Francisco of all places, where the increase of AIDS among gays was down to one percent five years ago. They're acting like it's Mardi Gras. Supposedly the most intelligent minority group in the country —

PAULY. Liz, Jews would have a fit if they heard you say that.

LIZ.   You don't deliberately stand in the path of a rushing train just because it might have brakes. AIDS is not some red badge of courage, not when it can be prevented. It's a badge of cowardliness, ignorance and lassitude.

PAULY.   How dare you say that! You've no idea the courage I've seen. They've earned the right to hope, damnit. You have no right to judge them!

LIZ.   I have every right! I saw it in Africa fifteen years ago. Shut up. Dozens of friends in Zaire, while I stood by helpless! I know perfectly well what you feel.

PAULY.   Fine, fine, fine.

LIZ.   — We didn't know back then that it could be prevented.

PAULY.   Liz, if they know what they're doing what can you do?

LIZ.   — They don't know shit. People do what their peers tell them to do. They do what's sexy. They're bored with using rubbers? Leather and rubber have a strong fetishistic appeal. Make the manufactures produce black rubbers and call them The Bastard. Put steel studs around them, French ticklers if you have to, *everyone* will want to get fucked with them. The point is —

PAULY.   I've taken your point, Liz. Make black condoms; steel studs, French ticklers. I think it's very hot. (*A chorus suddenly bursts out in full voice with the "Kyrie eleison" from Mozart's* Requiem.* *The organ behind the altar is featured for the first time. Pauly conducts a moment, singing along. Liz is gone.*) No, no, no, no. Darlings! Tenors. Please. "A." (*He hits an A on the piano.*) There is an "A" in there. (*He sings the phrase correctly.*) Take a break. Take five. Take ... whatever it takes. (*A dark bar, a jukebox is playing. Andy sits with Mickey who is about 30, Italian, happily drunk, in shirt and shorts. Mickey is completely unaware of his sex appeal.*)

MICKEY.   I mean she's the most beautiful girl in the world.

ANDY.   I know.

MICKEY.   She couldn't go out in the sun at all. Did you know that? Her skin was that white and delicate.

ANDY.   I heard that.

MICKEY.   Can you imagine what that does to a man? Skin like

* See Special Note on Songs and Recordings on copyright page.

24

that? I mean Benji was blonde all over. I mean *all over,* you know? You know what that means? To an *Italian?* I mean, Andy, she had *yellow eyes!*

ANDY. You're giving me an erection.

MICKEY. No, don't joke. That's why I love you. You can listen and — Aww, goddamnit, what is she trying to do? Make me not think? I can't help it if I look like a butcher, I got a *mind* in here. Is she trying to fuck me over?

ANDY. She said you looked like a butcher?

MICKEY. What? No, I said I look like a butcher. You think I don't know what I look like?

ANDY. You do look like a butcher.

MICKEY. I know. I said. You look at us, you wouldn't know we were geniuses. Who'd know?

ANDY. Are we geniuses?

MICKEY. You're definitely a genius and I do very, very competent work. Andy?

ANDY. Mickey?

MICKEY. What do you think I should do?

ANDY. Where'd she go?

MICKEY. Gone. Home to Amarillo maybe. She cleaned out the place. She must have hired a truck. She took the TV. There's just these little dust balls blowing around the floor where the TV was. You want to hear *irony?*

ANDY. So this is something she'd been planning.

MICKEY. — No, no, no, you want to hear irony? She left the VCR. I got no TV, I got a VCR.

ANDY. She leave a note? A letter?

MICKEY. Nope. Girl of few words.... Awww, Jesus, Andy, you know?

ANDY. I know.

BARTENDER. *(Calling from off.)* Fellas? Last call.

ANDY. Right.

MICKEY. *(Trying to remember an aphorism.)* "Of all the words, that were ever penned —" What is it? "Of all the words, great and small ..."

ANDY. Something like that.

MICKEY. "The saddest of all ..."

ANDY and MICKEY. "Last Call!"

MICKEY. Fucked that up. Like everything else.

ANDY. Come on. We're off that. *(Andy goes off to the bar. Barbara, Liz and Sue come out of the warehouse, closing the door, coming down front, looking out to the ocean, quietly drinking rather tall drinks in the moonlight. The interior of the church is faintly visible behind them.)*

SUE. I can't see you and Barbara's father together. I mean from what I've heard, I haven't met him. *(Behind them Don enters the church, begins setting up the altar.)*

LIZ. It seemed like the thing to do at the time. My downfall has always been men. It absolutely shakes me that every one comes equipped for my satisfaction. No amount of masturbation can replace the bastards. I'd schlepped Don over most of Africa, poor as church mice, living on his dad's army pension, working on my doctorate — Barbara's dad was stable; comfortable, caring.

BARBARA. Safe harbor. *(To Sue.)* Don's dad was a pilot in Vietnam. Early, before they even called them technical advisors. Tough act to follow.

LIZ. I don't know that we got along all that damn well either. He was off to 'Nam, back on leave. He was a career man, I was a kid, I wanted to finish school, get the hell out of here, hit the hills. We would never have seen each other. Come to think of it, if he hadn't got killed, we might have had the perfect marriage.

SUE. Liz, sometimes your cynicism really rocks me.

LIZ. Back somewhere in my childhood I thought the word marriage came from "mare." The old gray mare ain't what she used to be. Some broken-down, plodding, fucked-over brood horse. Lord I hate that word. I wasn't cut out to be married and have kids. It was just what we did back then. I hope you've learned that from me if nothing else.

BARBARA. Guaranteed. Whether I like it or not.

MICKEY. *(In the bar.)* Hey, it stopped raining.

ANDY. *(Entering with two beers.)* Too late for us.

SUE. It's stopped raining.

MICKEY. Can you hear the ocean?

26

SUE. *(At the same time.)* The ocean's furious tonight.

LIZ. I can't even see the damn ocean. Sounds very familiar. I have to get my glasses changed.

BARBARA. Don said your eyes are going.

MICKEY. I'm very drunk, you know that?

LIZ. They are.

ANDY. I know that.

MICKEY. Basically I've been drinking since ten this morning. How you doing?

ANDY. Not quite in your league, but getting there.

MICKEY. I'm not going to be able to work tomorrow night. Tonight. It is tomorrow.

ANDY. Sure you are.

MICKEY. Not my best. I want to do my best. I always do.

ANDY. I know.

MICKEY. *(Almost crying.)* I been waiting six months for this. We gotta *be* there, you know? And she pulls this.

BARBARA. It's never really lulled me, that sound. It's too damn big and profound. I'm not comfortable with it.

MICKEY. *(Suddenly bursts out bawling, as only an Italian man can blubber.)* WAAAAA! WAAAA!

ANDY. Come on, fella. Come on. Let's call it a nice warm night. You know? Get you home, get some sleep.

MICKEY. You going home?

ANDY. Going by the office, check out the stuff from Keck.

MICKEY. From where?

ANDY. Keck, Mickey. Hawaii.

MICKEY. I'm fucked up.

ANDY. You're fucked up.

MICKEY. Women don't know what they do to us. They don't know! They don't understand what we feel! You never hear about a woman going back to her estranged husband and blowing him and his new girlfriend away. Both the kids.

ANDY. Sure you do. What papers have you been reading?

MICKEY. No! Damnit! They don't have that horrible *thing* inside them, Andy, that can just snap. They don't know what they do to us!

ANDY. Don't kid yourself. They love it. *(Andy and Mickey leave*

27

the bar.)

LIZ. *(Getting up.)* It's getting cold. *(The women turn and go in. Carl stands at a server with his plate. Andy enters. Blaring sunrise. Carl is in a robe, Andy wears the same shorts, T-shirt and sandals.)*

CARL. Glad you took the time to dress, Andy.

ANDY. Carl, are you naked under that thing?

CARL. These are hot and she does them awfully well.

ANDY. It's going to be all I can do to watch you.

CARL. Orange juice?

ANDY. On top of beer? I don't think so.

CARL. You've not gone to bed. I'll assume this is your way of preparing for tonight's vigil.

ANDY. I was up with a sick friend. I'll have a coffee.

CARL. I'm afraid you might have to settle for tea.

ANDY. I'm fine.

CARL. I sense a lack of interest, Andy —

ANDY. It's not a meal that holds much fascination for me, Carl.

CARL. — In what I consider an extremely important test of these new computerized sensors. Who is this Bob in Hawaii and what is his level of competence? In your teaching assignments, in the popular lecture series you're giving under the college's umbrella. There was a certain British "It isn't done to try too hard" attitude at Oxford that got under my skin.

ANDY. Well, I try too hard and like it. Mickey can go to Hawaii if that would make you happier.

CARL. Oh, I've no complaints about Picco at all, very capable, very steady. Might have some inclination to concentrate now, without the distraction of that floozy. I understand the sculptress you're living with is in the School of Fine Arts this semester.

ANDY. And only this semester, I suspect, she doesn't like teaching. I like teaching, Carl. I can't say my students are over-prepared by the time I get them. Some are a little staggered by —

CARL. — Oh, and they love you. God knows you're the students' pet. They're perhaps not the best judge.

ANDY. Carl, you and I are very different. We're almost in different fields. If there was a way to have access to the cyclotron,

28

I'd probably be moonlighting as a particle physicist or scoping out neutrinos.

CARL. Oh, lord, let's be thankful for our shortcomings. What we don't need is Dr. Anderson spread even thinner. With your projects and your lectures and your articles, plus a substantial teaching workload and what is undoubtedly a chaotic private life.

ANDY. Private life?

CARL. People do talk.

ANDY. I've heard that.

CARL. Not I, Andy. I understand you have a comfortable enough place over by the country club. I've a number of business associates who've seen Barbara working there. Hideous work they say, but they're hardly critics. Dr. Smythe in the Art Department is quite taken with her. So is the Dean's wife, god help us.

ANDY. I don't know as it's much concern to our work.

CARL. I like to feel my people are comfortable, certainly.

ANDY. Snug as a bug. As a matter of fact we're pregnant.

CARL. Really. Andy. I had no idea.

ANDY. I thought probably you knew before I did.

CARL. I don't suppose that'll change your marital status, but certainly congratulations are in order.

ANDY. No, actually, we're debating whether or not to have the little bugger scraped out and flushed down the toilet. *(Carl edges his plate away.)* I'm sorry, I didn't mean to —

CARL. You lost last night to the weather, so you have only two nights now for this test and to get decent data for your black hole search. I imagine you'll be publishing something, you usually do. Be sure to run it by me before you send it off, right?

ANDY. Sure. If there's anything to see. Why?

CARL. I might be able to contribute something.

ANDY. To what? Holy shit. You want to be a co-author on it, don't you? You want your damn name on it.

CARL. Fairly standard practice, surely.

ANDY. This work is so preliminary, we're going to be analyzing data for months; it's damn unlikely they'll be anything to publish.

CARL. *(Getting up.)* You'll think of something. The sun is in the sky and the hour is pressing on. Just leave it with my girl. I'll see that it gets sent in.

ANDY. Carl, if something is appended to anything we write, I'll have to see it before it's sent anywhere.

CARL. That path over there leads right around the house to your car. *(He leaves Andy standing at the table. Andy turns to Liz, Barbara and Sue at the warehouse.)*

ANDY. What a day! Smell that air! And all those other things. At the crack of 9 A.M., having fulfilled my professional obligations, I presented myself, first customer of the day, to a sour-looking receptionist, in a bright wing of the inappropriately sterile Community Hospital. I filled out their six page form — bracingly presumptuous question, I might add — submitted to a blood test, was handed a small bottle, which I embraced, and a badly used copy of Hustler Magazine, which I arrogantly eschewed; and went into a quiet little room, fantasized glorious, immensely satisfying dreams, enormous breasts and pliant thighs, beat myself stupid, whooped for old glory, and shot my wad in the comforting test tube, it was more like, than a bottle.

BARBARA. You went to a sperm bank?!

ANDY. Mad impulse. Hedging my bets.

LIZ. A sperm bank counts as a sexual encounter, I'd think. Wouldn't you call that — scoring?

ANDY. Scoring? God! Winning the Series, the Super Bowl, the — my sports analogies are limited. Astronauts must feel like that at blast off. I think it was the most thoroughly satisfying sexual experience of my life.

BARBARA. You kill, right?

LIZ. If I'd known it was that exhilarating I'd have donated an egg or something while I still had one.

ANDY. Liz, you could cry! Thinking of all those women. Come to me! Bend to me! Want me! God it was primal. It was religious. And now — I'm going to bed.

LIZ. Have you been drinking? It's not 10 A.M.

ANDY. No, I just haven't had any sleep. Also for me it's very late at night. Also I don't have to get up till 4 in the afternoon.

30

Also I've been drinking.

BARBARA. The "Come to me, bend to me" gave it away, I think.

ANDY. Drinking and pondering. And I've come to the conclusion, that — Boy, I've tried, but I swear I don't know how you — what? How you *think.*

LIZ. If I were just starting my studies, that would be my field. The brain, cerebration. The brain isn't this perfect disinterested computer we pretend it is. Little pustules of inherited behavioral defenses keep popping up in the middle of what we'd like to think is pure reason. Not a clean machine, the brain.

ANDY. I meant — well, it sounds small now. I meant — I don't know how women think.

LIZ. Oh, good lord, Andy. Why are men always saying that? Women know perfectly well how men think.

ANDY. Not that it means a damn to you.

LIZ. I'd hope not. The woman holds the kid, the man holds the spear. That's all you have to know about the way women think.

BARBARA. Spear? What spear? That is such pure bullshit. You're always doing that. You don't know that.

LIZ. I beg your pardon but I do. The kid would play hell suckling his father.

BARBARA. There's such a thing as a bottle with a nipple on it now, mother. And formula. And a woman is perfectly capable of holding a spear.

LIZ. In most cultures women don't even know the mechanics of weapons.

BARBARA. Israel? China?

LIZ. We have very different agendas. Men and women aren't bonded to each other after all —

ANDY. The hell they're not.

LIZ. Of course they're not. If women are bonded to anything, they're bonded to their children. To protect the family, which is the only reason men and women hang together in the first place, a man uses brute strength and a woman uses — some brute. That should really start Barbara off.

BARBARA. No, say whatever you damn well want.

31

LIZ. So, that's everything you need to know about the way we think. Take an aspirin. Don't forget to shower.

BARBARA. There's too many instances of a mother raising her kids by herself for that to be even remotely —

LIZ. — Now? In this country? Tragedy of our times. The father abandons them, dies, is killed, or he disowns the child — or she might just have the good sense to take the kid and get out of there. You're only underlining my thesis.

SUE. Rather than hunting game, maybe men would have been better off sticking around the village eating corn cakes. Better for you than all that meat.

LIZ. I've noticed that about you, you always try to defuse an argument. What kind of lawyer would you have made? We're having fun. Actually wild game is very low in fat. Spa fare.

ANDY. We're just as bonded to our children as women are.

LIZ. What's wrong with you today? Your brain's gone to mush. Or alcohol. Mash.

ANDY. But it's basic instinct, you think, to have children.

LIZ. Oh, shut up. It's been debated whether we have any instincts at all.

ANDY. Then why would a mother want an abortion? Instead of having the baby? If it's so instinctive?

BARBARA. Where the hell are you coming from?

ANDY. I'm curious, okay? This is the woman's field, she knows this shit.

LIZ. I'm sorry. I didn't realize you were using me as a weapon against my daughter. You're not drunk at all. I never trust the word "baby" in a man's mouth. Say offspring or issue. "Baby" is one of those sweet-smelling, talcum powdered words with balloons and bows blowing all around it. A woman won't want to have a child, Andy, if she thinks she'll have need of both her arms. *(Turning to Barbara, quite angry.)* How did you let something like this happen?

BARBARA. Total accident.

LIZ. Oh, bullfeathers.

BARBARA. You're always saying that. It's horse feathers or bullshit.

·LIZ. Bullshit then. Why does he know?

BARBARA.   Mom, Andy and I understand each other very well on this. The doctor would have congratulated him anyway. Given him a cigar or some other phallic celebration.

LIZ.   You don't go to a doctor the man knows! This is all sounding willful.

BARBARA.   No, believe me. *(To Andy.)* We have both agreed we didn't want children. You can't even stay in the same house with a crying child, you walk straight out of the room. And so do I.

ANDY.   I don't. I didn't. Till it happened. Now it's happened. But if one little sperm got through all the barricades we threw up against it, it's got to be some kind of miracle. You should at least consider giving it a chance.

LIZ.   *(To Barbara.)* If you didn't want it, you should have taken care of it immediately.

ANDY.   She made the goddamned appointment before she even told me.

LIZ.   You just shush!

ANDY.   You still having fun?

LIZ.   Are you still talking?

ANDY.   I've got nothing to say in this, right? Isn't that the way it goes?

LIZ.   You've had your say, thank you.

ANDY.   The kid is mine too, Liz.

LIZ.   You don't know that!

BARBARA.   Mom! For godsake.

LIZ.   He doesn't know that, thank you. Golfers and young muscle-building caddies wander by every five minutes. She's a magnificent woman! Working outside with huge masses of wood, sheets of metal, banging away, drawing a crowd, who knows who could come by.

ANDY.   That's really low, Liz.

LIZ.   That's the truth! You may go. We don't need you here.

ANDY.   You're who we don't need here. You guys are really something. You make me physically sick, you know that? *(He leaves.)*

BARBARA.   I know the feeling!

LIZ.   Barbara, shut up. Never pay any attention to what a man

33

says when he's leaving the room. I don't see how you can possibly have children at this point in your life. You can bring the child to issue for adoption, you'd never have to see it, or you can take care of it now. Those are your options.

SUE. I can think of at least four others.

LIZ. You're not an artist.

BARBARA. Mom has this romantic nineteenth century notion that artists don't live normal healthy lives.

LIZ. I've no truck with what people call healthy or normal. Yes, I believe society crushes individuality. Oh, big revelation, Liz. What do you intend to do?

SUE. Your own example would have spoiled your thesis.

LIZ. What?

SUE. About a mother being bonded to her child. You said the father might be unknown, or leave, or die, or be killed, the parents might get a divorce. You didn't say the mother could just split without the kid. You know, abandon the child. Like you did Barbara. *(The sound of an elevator is heard. Control Room of the Observatory. Mickey is at the observer's console. The room is represented by a large table with several TV monitors. A window might show the huge telescope in the adjoining observatory. There is a pounding on the door.)*

MICKEY. Hold it a second. *(Going to the door.)* Where you been, slack-ass. Oh, sorry. *(They all crowd into the space, all wear heavy coats, they are taking off hats, etc.)*

DON	PAULY	MICKEY
Hi. It's Mickey, isn't it?	Hi, Mickey. It is bitter out there. Brrrr.	God, wait! We can't have have visitors up here at night. What's going on?

SUE. *(Crowding in.)* Where's Andy? Hi.

DON. We didn't see Andy's car, is he here? Didn't he warn you?

MICKEY. I'm sorry. What's up? No, he didn't tell me anything. He isn't here yet.

DON. He said give you one night to get straightened out, then come on up.

MICKEY. You're Barbara's step-brother, the priest, I've met —

DON. — Half brother, maternal brother.

MICKEY. Father uh —

DON. Don. Please.

MICKEY. I'm sorry, I didn't recognize you without the vestments.

DON. You know Sue Olmsted? Mickey Picco, Andy's partner.

MICKEY. No. Hi. I'm pleased to meet you, but —

DON. Sue's working with my mother. And Pauly Scott.

MICKEY. Hi, yeah, I think we've —

PAULY. — Many times, with Barbara and Andy. Hi.

MICKEY. Oh. Yeah. I remember, with the queer choir.

DON. We wanted to see where you guys penetrate the mysteries. Andy said come on up.

MICKEY. You shouldn't have come up that road in this weather.

PAULY. *(Looking through the window.)* Tell me about it. Wow, look at that mother.

SUE. Is that the actual telescope in there?

MICKEY. Yeah. You can't go in there! We can't have warm air in the observatory. How did you get up the mountain?

PAULY. Father Don has 4-wheel drive.

SUE. And, I'm sorry, but a damned chancy heater.

PAULY. It is brutal out there.

SUE. Andy said it wouldn't be what we expected.

MICKEY. And it isn't, right? Don't touch that console! Sorry.

SUE. I'm freezing my buns off.

MICKEY. Maybe it's cold in this room, I can turn the heat up in here.

DON. If Andy's not going to be here, we shouldn't stay.

MICKEY. No, it's just — I'm not gonna chase you out, Christ, it takes an hour and a half to get up here. Warm up at least.

PAULY. So. What have we got?

MICKEY. Uh…. Well … this is the controller's console.

PAULY. That's you?

MICKEY. Usually. It's all automated. You just type in declination and right ascension and the telescope moves into position.

SUE. Cool.

MICKEY.   Observer's console. *(With a chart.)* This is our finding chart. That's what we're looking at this run. Keck did a run last night. Totally useless. Some bug in their equipment. Bob's been checking it out all day.

DON.   And you're at the mercy of the weather, aren't you?

MICKEY.   The weather, instruments, and you don't get another chance, time's booked a year in advance.

PAULY.   *(Back to the monitor.)* Does this display? I mean, will we actually see pictures of a star or whatever it is?

MICKEY.   No. It's digital, you'd see columns of numbers. *(Cheerily helpful.)* You can come back during visitor's hours, they give tours of the telescope, you can walk all around it. *(They are engrossed with the equipment.)* Uh. You guys want some soup, coffee?

PAULY.   We stuffed ourselves on the way up. *(There is a beep from the observer's console.)*

DON.   What's that?

MICKEY.   *(Moves to the console, typing.)* Let me clear a couple of megabytes from my disk. This is coming in from Keck. This is the one he screwed up last night. OK, that's a z equals five. It may not look like much but nobody's ever taken this spectrum before.

SUE.   That's a spectrum? It really is just numbers.

MICKEY.   Yeah. Tells us what it's made of. Oh, goddamn.

SUE.   What?

MICKEY.   *(Pause. Looking at screen.)* We're gonna have to do this over, something fucked up. Excuse the language.

PAULY   SUE   DON.
Think nothing of it.   Don't mind me.   It's all right.

MICKEY.   *(Resetting the computers.)* Shit. Sorry. Where the hell's Andy? This is what makes our job really fun. What the — I asked it to measure the ratio of the equivalent widths, which is what was wrong last night. Two of the oxygen lines — it's an easy way to see if you've got something like a clean — Damn.

SUE.   You have to do it again? *(Whispered to Don.)* We should go.

MICKEY.   *(Playing with the keys.)* Yeah. We're gonna have to check everything out and run it again. Hawaii's got a storm coming this morning. Great.

PAULY. What ratio are you checking?

MICKEY. Two of the oxygen absorption lines. Which are always the same. They're the same in every star, they're the same if you're looking at a light bulb.

PAULY. What is it supposed to be?

MICKEY. Five. Always.

SUE. What did you get?

MICKEY. Fourteen.

PAULY. Shit.

MICKEY. Yeah. That's a little wide for instrument error.

PAULY. Are there any ratios that great? I mean I don't know what you're talking about but —

MICKEY. No, Pauly, there are no ratios that great. *(Moving to the other console.)* Well, to hell with it, you know? Let *them* worry about it. We're here to test a lot of damn important equipment on our own telescope. That's enough to deal with. Did Andy tell you we've been installing these really cool computer sensors and photo —

PAULY. Yeah he told us, it's great —

MICKEY. It's gonna boost the capacity more than double. That's what we should worry about. *(Punching keys on the console.)* This should be long enough. Let's see what we've got.

SUE. This is the same object as Keck?

MICKEY. Yeah, only maybe we got it right. *(Pointing to the console.)* See? All of that for a screen full of numbers. We store that, and go on to the next coordinates. We've gotta do all four tonight. Study them tomorrow, next week, next month. Now, I type in the next coordinates. OK, guys, you'll get a kick out of this. *(The telescope in the other room moves, the entire ceiling of the observatory rotates with a grinding noise.)*

SUE. All right!

MICKEY. I thought you'd like that. So this is what I do all night. End of demonstration. Wasn't that exciting? *(Looking at the console.)* This is looking really good, near as I can tell the equipment here is working great. I can bring up the spectrum — *(Typing.)* There. So — *(He stares at the screen, then looks back and forth from console to console, stunned. What he sees is impossible.*

Only gradually does he realize there are others in the room.)

PAULY. What? *(Mickey doesn't hear.)* What?

MICKEY. *(Coming out of it. Covering.)* Look, guys this is fun with all of you here, but —

SUE. — Yeah, we're in the way here —

MICKEY. — This is all new stuff, I have to mess with things, jiggle things around, call a few people, I'm gonna need some breathing-room or elbow-room or something here. No joke, Okay? I may be on this all night.

DON. Sure. We'd better head back down the mountain. I wish we could help, but obviously we can't.

PAULY. I'll gladly stay.

SUE. You really are incorrigible.

PAULY. I mean if I can help. This is fascinating.

MICKEY. Thanks, but I'm probably just messing up. I'm about to go non-linear here.

DON. Go what?

MICKEY. Non-linear. Never mind. *Sue* can stay.

SUE. I'll stay.

DON. I don't think so.

SUE. I'll stay if it'll help.

PAULY. I don't think I've seen you with a straight man yet who didn't hit on you.

SUE. *(Not necessarily happy about it.)* I know.

MICKEY. I was joking, Sue, I'm sorry. I'm nervous.

DON. It's probably just us.

MICKEY. No, no. If you see Andy tell him to get his ass up here. Thank you. All. Really. I'm sorry if it wasn't very —

SUE. No, thank you. Good luck.

DON. *(At the same time.)* I hope the screw-up wasn't anything we did.

MICKEY. No way.

PAULY. *(Same time.)* We'll find Andy.

SUE. *(As the elevator doors close.)* I didn't even get warm.

MICKEY. Yeah, bye bye. And good…. *(Looking at the screen.)* What the hell are you supposed to mean?

ANDY. *(Entering from the other direction.)* What have we got?

MICKEY. How long you been out there?

ANDY. I was just behind them on the freeway, I missed the exit, my mind was on something else. What have we got?

MICKEY. Same as last night. On both telescopes. Keck and here.

ANDY. That's not possible.

MICKEY. I know.

ANDY. Did you estimate the continuum level?

MICKEY. Yeah. Maybe I screwed up. You do it. *(Andy punches some keys on the console.)*

ANDY. I get the same thing. This is our telescope?

MICKEY. Yeah.

ANDY. Clear as a bell.

MICKEY. Yeah, equipment works great, clear as a bell and exactly the same as Keck. Only as you said that's impossible.

ANDY. Mickey, get Hawaii for me. *(They look at each other. Mickey picks up the phone, dials three numbers.)* Yeah, Bob, we're going on to the next group. G1083. That's right. Well, we'll see. If the next one does this, something is definitely strange. N019 — G1083 You got it?

MICKEY. *(Looking at the screen.)* Boy you guys sure are beautiful, but what the hell are you? *(The lecture hall. Andy turns to his audience. The lights go out on the rest of the stage. The house lights might sneak up to the position they were in at the top of the act.)*

ANDY. I called up someone and asked her to be here today because she asked me when I first became interested in astronomy and I said I'd always been. Then, afterwards, I realized that wasn't true at all. I could pin-point the moment exactly.

When I was a kid we lived in Philadelphia and for a while my mother's sister lived there too. Mother was just a mother, and a fine one, but Aunt Julia was extraordinary. She was quite a brilliant mathematician, had written the definitive work on minus numbers. And Aunt Julia used to take me places. Museums, the movies, lectures — every Friday. This was for her, you understand, this was not for me. I pleaded not to go.

She held my hand, very tightly, painfully tightly, and dragged me all over Philly, Camden, Rutgers. March time. She was going to expose this kid to culture if it killed him.

39

She took me to completely incomprehensible movies. For a kid of six and a half? She was crazy about Japanese Art Films, the ones that are not about the samurai. And *The Blue Angel.* In German. The symphony and opera. I don't remember any of the places she took me before my fifth birthday. Maybe that was our first outing. Because on my fifth birthday — she took me to the planetarium.

I don't know how you remember things. I have no memory of anything at all for the first four years of my life ... and nearly total recall of every moment after that.

The lights went out in the planetarium ... dimmed dramatically. And a man's voice, like Orson Wells, amplified, echoing, mysterious said ... *(In the voice.)*

"This is the World we live in. This is the Universe we live in." *(A glowing map of the night sky begins to appear all across the back wall, the ceiling and walls of the theater.)*

Jesus!

I remember every word of that lecture still. It was quite foolish and romantic and totally superficial. No matter. That's where my life began.

I was born in the Fels Planetarium in the Franklin Institute, in Philadelphia, Pennsylvania, at the age of five.

And my life was mapped out for me from that moment. It was as clear to me as the night sky who I was and what road I had to take.

Jesus! Imagine it. *(In awe.)*

"This is the world we live in!"

END OF ACT ONE

40

ACT TWO

The church garden. Don and Liz. Don is drinking red wine. Pauly is rehearsing the "Dies irae" section of Mozart's Requiem* *inside. It is sounding quite good. Liz and Don listen a moment. The requiem continues under the scene.*

LIZ. That's actually sounding pretty darn fair.

DON. He'll get it out of them.

LIZ. If it's there to get.

DON. If it's there or not. And probably it is. Unlike — *(Annoyed.)* I've been talking for a few months with an architect, a couple of doctors, a group of health care workers. We're thinking that old garage, we used to keep the school buses in, big brick barn of a thing, isn't it? It's only for storage now. I feel it could be better used as a hospice. Run by the church, maybe in partnership with St. Andrew's R. C.

LIZ. You're thinking AIDS patients?

DON. Anyone. Well, in this neighborhood it'd be mostly AIDS patients. We may be a stylish ghetto, but we're basically poor. There are a lot of people here who've never had insurance, or never worked at all.

LIZ. "Self-employed."

DON. Or had some schlock insurance company stiff them. Or never worked for a company. Housewives, hustlers.

LIZ. Same thing.

DON. Runaways, artists, actors. Little theaters, some of the not-for-profit institutions, exploit their people shamelessly. Small dance companies, *churches.* A lot of people, essentially, are life-time volunteers. *(Beat.)* With all the changes, people beginning to believe they may actually live, hospices closing for lack of patients, hospitals cutting down on their AIDS wards. You want to be there for the — *(For want of a better expression.)* — ones that fall.

---

* See Special Note on Songs and Recordings on copyright page.

LIZ.   Are you drinking too much?

DON.   Uh…. Probably. Is that a comment on the possibility of making a hospice here?

LIZ.   No, you'd be good in a hospice.

DON.   I think so. Unfortunately the board was horrified. I met with them last night. They were soundly adamant. Well, they felt blindsided. They said everything short of "We're not our brother's keeper."

LIZ.   You need their approval?

DON.   Mom. I need their approval to piss. Of course I need their approval, they'd be running it.

LIZ.   Do it anyway, go over their heads.

DON.   It got very hot. Two of them loved the idea; the other seven said we had a martyr complex. They couldn't afford it, couldn't administer, how would you heat it, any excuse. Idiots. *(Liz has closed her eyes.)* Are you all right?

LIZ.   Headache. Nothing. Will they come around?

DON.   Oh…. A guarded "probably." I didn't go about it — You have to let them think it's their idea. I get impatient with that kind of politics.

LIZ.   I've always thought you were pretty good at manipulating people.

DON.   Is that supposed to be a compliment?

LIZ.   Of course it is.

DON.   I am, actually.

LIZ.   It's why you're good at your job. Only don't become a drunken priest, it's too cliched. *(Instant shift.)* I've discovered *recorded books* for the seeing impaired. They've recorded all the wrong books, but still it's a blessing.

DON.   *(A bit confused by the shift.)* Can you read at all?

LIZ.   If the letters are two inches high. Last week I could read headlines. Now, it would have to be one hell of a *banner* headline: DEMOCRATS RETAKE THE SOUTH!

DON.   Can you watch TV?

LIZ.   Who would want to?

DON.   Well, the news.

LIZ.   That's not the news. A couple burned in a fire, a mother beat her child to death. They should come on the news and say, "Well, today, there are still more people in the world than the rich people need to maintain their wealth." And that would be the end of it. "We'll check it out tomorrow, if anything changes, we'll let you know."

DON. "Back to our regularly scheduled program."

LIZ. Barbara says you're going straight. What's that?

DON. No. That's just Pauly talking. She told me she thought you were glad I didn't marry so you wouldn't have to share me.

LIZ. Whatever makes you happy. If your living with Pauly didn't bother me, I'm not going to be upset about you going with women.

DON. I don't have time for it and it takes time. I think I'm moving toward none of it. That's what I'm comfortable with.

LIZ. Celibacy? God help us.

DON. My feelings are just more generalized lately — moving away from the specific sex-object to the general — *(For want of a better phrase.)* — welfare of the flock. Yeah, celibacy. It's not that difficult.

LIZ. And you've inherited your dad's huge dick too.

DON. Mom!

LIZ. What a waste. How do you do it? Keep up any enthusiasm for helping people?

DON. I thought I got it from you.

LIZ. I've never done anything of the sort. No. You've gone way past me. You and Barbara, both of you. It's dangerous, but I think that's the point.

DON. Of what?

LIZ. Well, you. You've become the Shaman.

DON. I don't quite think of myself like that. With feathers and gourd rattlers?

LIZ. With whatever is the traditional, accepted, equivalent.

DON. I think a Shaman would have better control of his board. No. I did, actually.

LIZ. Did what?

DON. Went over their heads. I called the Bishop, laid it out for him, he thinks it's a splendid idea.

LIZ. I thought you said the Bishop wanted in your pants.

DON. Different Bishop.

LIZ.   What does this one look like?

DON.   Out of the question. He looks too much like you.

LIZ.   Oh, poor man. Not a chance in hell.

DON.   I still have to think of a way to ease the board into liking it.

LIZ.   Well, that's what I'm saying, damnit. Don't ease. Scare the bastards. Fire and brimstone. Instill the fear of God, then exploit it for everything it's worth. Money and death, honey. It's all about money and fear of dying. A good leader knows how to make people pay for what they believe in.

DON.   You really are the devil.

LIZ.   I try. *(From the church, the music stops mid-phrase as they exit.)*

PAULY.   *(Off.)* Stop, stop. Thank you. You are Gentlemen and Gentle Ladies of exceedingly fine quality. *(An Italian restaurant — A large table is set for six. A side table carries a carafe of red wine. Sue and Mickey, the first to arrive, each have a glass of wine they will finish shortly. Faint noises from the bar.)*

SUE.   I don't trust scientists, or a lot of scientists, they give me the crawlies. It's just ignorance, but I mean — the *gene splices,* genetic engineering, from what I've read, that really —

MICKEY.   — Oh, man. The gene-benders. They are into some scary shit.

SUE.   Governments must be salivating.

MICKEY.   I'm a long way from convinced they don't all have a Master Race Agenda tucked away somewhere.

SUE.   The scientists or the Governments?

MICKEY.   Probably both. And most of the Fortune 500, who really run the country.

SUE.   Thank god. A fellow paranoid.

MICKEY.   No way. That stuff is scary.

SUE.   I'd feel a lot easier if I had *in my hands* a psychological profile of ever biologist working on that stuff.

MICKEY.   — They've got the power. They've got the power. Let's hope they have the sense to sit on it.

SUE.   You're joking. Just knowing and not using it isn't power.

MICKEY.   "Power" is what, though? Legally?

SUE.   The same as anywhere else. Probably: The ability to effect a change.

44

MICKEY. Yeah, but "ability." I'm thinking like it's enough to know you have it and not use it. Like millionaires hoarding stolen paintings in their cellars.

SUE. Bullshit, Mickey. The magic wand isn't magic under your pillow. One of those suckers is going to say, this isn't of *benefit* to mankind unless I tell —

MICKEY. — Oh, god, you're right, I hate it. For the sake of the species. It starts out curing cancer and ends —

SUE. — And ends up creating a whole race of wasteoids. *(Looking around.)* Where is everybody?

MICKEY. All this paranoia is making me very thirsty. *(Sue goes to the tray of wine and brings it to the table.)*

SUE. I ordered another carafe while you were in the john.

MICKEY. I don't think I've ever had a girl — woman order for me before.

SUE. Well this girl woman is very thirsty. So. Did you get your problem straightened out?

MICKEY. Uh ... *(Blank beat.)* I'm sorry, I suddenly realized I have so many problems I don't know which one you're talking about.

SUE. With the computer. At the observatory. Pauly was thrilled out of his gourd. I mean to me it just looked like your basic fuck-up, but he was revved.

MICKEY. Oh, god, no. He's gonna spread it all over town. You can't say anything. I mean nothing at all.

SUE. What? You think because he's gay, he's a gossip?

MICKEY. Yes.

SUE. Shame on you. He swore us all to secrecy.

MICKEY. Yeah, but see, even that is admitting there's something there.

SUE. So what have you got?

MICKEY. We have no idea. And I shouldn't even tell you we have no idea. Ninety-nine percent it's just an equipment error. Or human error, or we're not understanding something. We're not talking about it.

SUE. Wow. That good.

MICKEY. No, that uncertain. Andy's checking out some things. He's probably shot it down by now.

SUE.   Don't you have an uncertainty law or hypothesis in physics?

MICKEY.   Heisenberg's Uncertainty Principle. Only this is uncertain in the sense that we don't know what the hell it is we're looking at. I mean *at all.*

SUE.   Great. So I saw Mickey Picco discover something that nobody had ever seen before.

MICKEY.   More like observe something that can not possibly exist in the universe as we know it.

SUE.   Whoa.

MICKEY.   Yeah. *(Seeing Andy.)* Oh, shit. Don't say anything to Andy. We were talking about the weather —

SUE.   We are not. *(Andy joins them, sitting between them. He is boiling angry.)*

ANDY.   You're not going to believe this one.

MICKEY.   You hear from Farnov?

ANDY.   Yeah. Forgive me, Sue. I'm sorry, I am burning on this one. I'm sitting at the console, F. T. P'ed the spectrum from Farnov. Carl comes in. Like: "What's happening?"

MICKEY.   Oh, god.

ANDY.   He's looking at the screen, says, What's that? I say I asked a friend to take the spectrum of a quasar z=5. "Why?"

MICKEY.   So he had to know the whole thing.

ANDY.   Sorry, Sue.

SUE.   No, it has you steamed. What? *(Andy looks at Mickey, looks off to the bar. Mickey and Andy agree to tell her.)*

ANDY.   OK. The other night while you were up at the observatory, we got an anomalous spectrum. To see if it was in error, I asked a friend of mine at another observatory to do us a favor, take a spectrum, just send it to us.

SUE.   So he did and F. T. P'ed it to you. Scientific e-mail.

ANDY.   Right. We've been working on this steady for sixty hours. I haven't been home. I haven't left the office. The more we examine this, the crazier it gets.

MICKEY.   Totally off the charts.

ANDY.   Entirely new physics. Mickey, Farnov's observation was identical.

MICKEY.   *(Overjoyed.)* Ahhhh! *(Looks around.)* Shit. Oh, man! I can't believe it. I didn't make a mistake, you didn't make a mistake, it's really there.

ANDY. It's really there. I show Carl, I say I'm sending a telegram.

MICKEY. You sent the telegram?!

ANDY. No.

MICKEY. Carl.

ANDY. Wants to go over the data.

MICKEY. Most cautious chicken-shit on God's earth.

ANDY. Doesn't want us to make fools of the school.

MICKEY. When?

ANDY. Carl's call. No later than tomorrow. Crack of dawn. Sorry, Sue.

SUE. That's OK. That's great.

MICKEY. How much have you had to drink?

ANDY. A couple of pints.

SUE. Why send a telegram?

ANDY. If you discover something, a nova, comet, you send a telegram to the Astronomy Society.

SUE. You claim it.

MICKEY. Right. This is amazing.

ANDY. It is, it could be. If that bastard doesn't — to hell with it. What were you two talking about when I so rudely? I thought I heard my name.

MICKEY. Who remembers.

SUE. Mickey was trying to explain Heisenberg's Uncertainty Principle. You do it, you make that stuff seem easy. *(To Mickey.)* I went to one of his lectures; which was great, except he delivered the entire lecture to me. Completely forgetting he's living with a genius who happens to be pregnant. It was very weird.

MICKEY. Boy, are you slick.

SUE. Comes from being an only child.

MICKEY. Wait. Pregnant? You and Barbara?

ANDY. Looks that way.

MICKEY. That's great.

ANDY. I'm still trying to get my mind around it. An artist mother, a scientist dad, the kid will probably turn out to be Martina Hingis. Neither one of us will understand a word she's

47

saying.

MICKEY.   Isn't that always the way.

ANDY.   Start right now, saving for tennis camp or whatever.

MICKEY.   Daddy.

ANDY.   Don't talk about it. I can't think about it. *(Pauly joins them. He carries a martini, kisses Sue on the cheek in passing.)*

PAULY.   Hi guys, and don't say it.

SUE.   Happy birthday. You're late. You're never late.

PAULY.   I was sitting at the bar watching you two. Thirty years old. *(Lying, bitter.)* It hasn't bothered me yet.

SUE.   How's Mozart's requiem coming?

PAULY.   You're not going to believe this but it's almost sounding like music.

ANDY.   Pauly. Heisenberg's Uncertainty Principle. You still remember that one?

PAULY.   Please. I studied basic physics. I thought I saw an analogy between science and music. I was younger then.

ANDY.   Sue wants to know.

PAULY.   The entire physics department of Stanford University is sitting at the bar, ask one of them. Trust me, it does not effect the world we live in.

ANDY.   Are you sure?

PAULY.   Andy, never question me, I fall completely apart. *(To Sue, quite rapidly.)* The Uncertainty Principle says that on the sub-atomic level it's impossible to measure the position and speed of a particle at the same time. You can measure the speed or determine the position but not both simultaneously. And if you try to measure them the act of tinkering with them actually fucks up their behavior, which is really spooky. So essentially the Uncertainty Principle says on the sub-atomic scale we can never really know dick. At least with any certainty. You feeling better now?

SUE.   I knew I'd wish I hadn't asked.

ANDY.   On the large scale, in the real world, you can have a bus schedule. On the sub-atomic level you can't have a bus schedule.

SUE.   So you really *don't* know dick.

ANDY.   Don't let that get around.

MICKEY. Anything else you wanted to ask me?

SUE. One or two maybe. *(Liz and Don join them and take a seat. The men stand, Pauly first.)*

LIZ. Are we late?

SUE. Mickey and I were incredibly early. I've got kind of a buzz on, are you feeling that?

MICKEY. Feeling something. Can you think? I've lost my ability to think.

ANDY. Me too.

LIZ. Do you have a pad with you? I know it's not office hours but I forget everything.

SUE. Your retention is phenomenal.

LIZ. They won't stand for a tape recorder, they actually frisked me once to see if I was wired. Make a note: "Knock" means "Chump" or "Fallguy" and — what did I say?

DON. "Need" means doctor. N-E-E-D as in needle, syringe.

LIZ. Doctor, nurse, parole officer, social worker, minister, any of the do-gooders. I finally convinced them I wasn't a Need. This place is a dump, why haven't you brought me here before?

ANDY. All the Astrophysicist nerds in the Bay Area come here.

DON. Does that answer your question?

MICKEY. They give you a lot of food and it's cheap.

ANDY. And good.

MICKEY. And good.

ANDY. So how is it going in Gangland?

LIZ. They're all beyond me, Andy. I'd be as good talking to the Martians.

ANDY. There'll be a shuttle leaving for Mars any day now.

LIZ. Why don't you guys leave exploitation of the planets to machines? Whatever they're looking for, they're not going to find it in the stars, you'll find it in the bars sooner.

ANDY. *(With an edge.)* Maybe you should go tell NASA what makes people tick.

LIZ. They'd be a lot better off with a few anthropologists than all those fucking psychiatrists. If you want people in space you'd better drug them or something.

MICKEY.   I think they plan on freezing them.

LIZ.   Good. Where do I sign up for the trip? I'm doing next to nothing here.

ANDY.   And some things are found in the stars, Liz.

LIZ.   Are you OK? *(This last to Barbara as she joins them. She is tired and out of it.)*

BARBARA.   I'm fine. *(Hello.)* Everybody.

LIZ.   Should you be here?

BARBARA.   Probably not. I've just been working, I'm OK. Happy birthday, Pauly. Or are we saying that?

PAULY.   No, I'm being very pragmatic today.

BARBARA.   It's a day for it.

SUE.   How's the liver?

BARBARA.   *What?*

SUE.   How is the liver here?

DON.   I was just going to ask.

BARBARA.   Oh. God.

ANDY.   I haven't had it.

MICKEY.   I haven't had it.

ANDY.   *(To Barbara.)* Incredible, incredible news.

BARBARA.   What?

ANDY.   Tomorrow. Worth waiting for.

BARBARA.   I hate that. Don't tell me there's incredible news unless you're prepared to tell me what it is.

MICKEY.   Holy shit! What's he doing here?

ANDY.   *(Seeing Carl.)* Fuck, fuck, fuck a duck. Say nothing about nothing. I don't believe he has the nerve to — See how long it takes him to tell you he went to Oxford. He.... *(Andy shuts up as Carl enters, unexpected, surprised to see so many people. Mickey and Andy rise.)*

CARL.   Mickey, Andy. What a surprise.

ANDY.   How the hell did you find us, Carl?

CARL.   I hope this isn't a celebration. That might be premature.

LIZ.   Why? It is, of sorts.

CARL.   *(Skeptical.)* I see. May I ask the occasion?

SUE.   It's Pauly's thirtieth birthday.

PAULY.   I'm being very strong.

ANDY. Crazy about your trust, Carl. Everyone, this is Dr. Carl Conklin White, our boss. I didn't know you came here.

CARL. Oh, yes.

MICKEY. *(Whispered to Sue.)* Never seen him here once.

ANDY. *(Over Mickey.)* This is Dr. Elizabeth Barnard, Barbara's mother.

CARL. Dr. Barnard I'm honored.

ANDY. You know Barbara —

BARBARA. Carl.

ANDY. Liz's assistant, Sue Olmsted. Barbara's brother, Father Don Walker, pastor of the Second Episcopal Church, better known as the Gay Cathedral.

PAULY. You are such an ass.

ANDY. And Pauly Scott, the choir master there.

CARL. Pleased to meet you.

PAULY. Your boys were saying when you came in that they hoped you'd join us. *(Andy glares at him.)*

CARL. Well, then…. Maybe I will. I have no interest in anything whatever except my two cohorts in crime here. Actually, I was lying, I was hoping I'd see you. I don't suppose you've thought about anything else all afternoon. I know I haven't. I've just come from a meeting with the president of the university. I was completely incoherent, he must have thought I was drunk.

BARBARA and DON. What?

ANDY. I think we've reached some kind of critical mass here.

CARL. You'll have to forgive us, none of us can be expected to be himself tonight.

MICKEY. I'm making it an early evening, guys.

CARL. Oh, yes, I think so. If any of us can sleep.

LIZ. May we ask?

ANDY. I think, no, you better not ask. And we better not say any more.

PAULY. Oh, please. You've obviously found something fantastic.

CARL. *(Pleasantly.)* I don't think I like this young man. Pauly, we don't have any idea, not a clue. Well, actually, nothing but ideas and clues. Too many.

ANDY.   Carl.

SUE.   You've heard the big bang.

CARL.   No, no, we heard that years ago.

PAULY.   *(To Sue.)* Not the bang, but the residual noise it left, still out there humming away.

CARL.   I see we're going to have to be very circumspect around this one. Yes, we are excited. It's safe to say I won't be looking at our local galaxy group for a while.

ANDY.   You have to understand Professor White is a total aesthete.

CARL.   God knows I've never made any bones about it. I'm looking for beauty and symmetry. And current thought possess neither.

MICKEY.   Professor White has picked up Einstein's torch.

CARL.   Dr. Einstein's torch was never dropped, Picco. But, yes, the simplicity that he sought in — *(Suddenly to Barbara.)* Good lord! I have to tell you, I saw your show. I'd read the most ghastly reports. Actually I was in the neighborhood and went to scoff. I think your work is superb. It's extraordinary. I'm not myself, I should have said that the moment I saw you.

ANDY.   Isn't she astonishing?

PAULY.   *(Over.)* Isn't it great?

BARBARA.   Thank you.

CARL.   Doctor Smythe says I'm to use my powers of persuasion to encourage you to stay with his department for another semester, I hope you will.

BARBARA.   Thanks but — There's a young woman that's very promising, but I doubt it.

CARL.   That one should be all you need.

BARBARA.   I'm working pretty furiously right now. We'll see, unlikely.

CARL.   I haven't entreated you yet — I can be very persuasive. *(To Andy.)* Yes, I am, Andy. I make no apologies for being an aesthete. Aesthetics and science have always been symbiotic binaries. *(To the others.)* What scientists are searching for, have been for decades — at least cosmologists and particle physicists — what we dream of finding one day is — *(Ever the professor.)* What? Anyone? Not Pauly, he seems to know this. *(Andy gets up*

and abruptly leaves the table, going to the bar.)
DON.   A unified theory.
SUE.   *(Over.)* The Theory of Everything.
CARL.   Exactly. "The Theory of Everything." Thank god for bright young people —
PAULY.   Everyone in the world read Hawkings' book.
CARL.   Everyone in the world *bought* Hawkings' book. Those that read it — I was in London, lord what a fuss the poor London literati were raising. They're appalled at the thought anyone but they should venture an opinion on the nature of the world, even one of their own. They despise scientists and always have. Or certainly distrust us.
LIZ.   I don't think despise is too strong a word.
CARL.   And they're woefully ignorant; on science, religion, philosophy.
LIZ.   Psychology, behavior, the arts.
DON.   Mother is badly received there too.
LIZ.   I've reared an ingrate.
CARL.   They're very good on literature.
LIZ.   English literature. Totally unread in contemporary world literature.
CARL.   That's absolutely true; more cloistered than the Germans.
LIZ.   The Germans *read!*
CARL.   I love bashing the British.
LIZ.   Well, they're so damn self-satisfied.
PAULY.   I don't believe a word of it.
SUE.   You're dealing with a massive Anglophile here. *(Andy returns with a whiskey and another carafe of red wine. He sits down, glaring at Carl.)*
LIZ.   And these two guys have found that?
CARL.   Found what, Dr. Barnard?
LIZ.   A standard model; a theory of everything.
CARL.   Oh, good god no. But it's been postulated that the universe might have been created to contain several vacuum "domains" or parallel universes, not just the one we know. And it's possible that the realization of the laws of physics might be very different from our own domain in some of the others.

ANDY. Carl, goddamnit, have you been drinking?

CARL. One sherry, which I'm sure leaves me in your dust.

ANDY. We haven't seen into another universe or "domain," Carl.

MICKEY. The wall between domains would contain enormous energy — you could never see through it. Not this easily.

ANDY. *(Overlapping.)* Never. Never see through it.

CARL. *(To the others.)* You see what it is. We know nothing. Suffice to say, what my guys have found throws one hell of a wrench in the Big Boys' quantum mechanics.

MICKEY. More than likely it wouldn't effect quantum mechanics at all.

ANDY. *Maybe* not. Shut-up about it.

CARL. This is completely *entre nous,* you understand. I think Andy feels I shouldn't have said this much.

LIZ. Of course.

CARL. Lord, it's getting late. I may not be able to stay for dinner, I have to be at a meeting in Denver tomorrow.

ANDY. I'll go, I'd love to get the hell out of here.

CARL. No, no, it's Heads of Departments. Just a mutual congratulations on the triumph of science and engineering over ignorance and superstition.

LIZ. You mean that ironically, of course.

CARL. *(Struck.)* Not altogether, I hope. I loathe all this traveling. The last place I want to be is anywhere away from here.

SUE. What is our "local galaxy group"?

CARL. Beg pardon, Miss Olmsted? Any relation to the landscape architect, Frederick Law Olmsted?

SUE. Dad was a great-great something or other. You said you won't be looking at our local galaxy group for a while.

MICKEY. That's Professor White's field.

CARL. That's my bivouac just now. Since Oxford actually.

SUE. Eleven minutes.

LIZ. You're sure you're all right?

BARBARA. Fine. Tired.

CARL. — Galaxies are grouped, and rotate around a common center. Our group is 23 galaxies that are part of a super cluster of groups rotating around its common center. *(He looks at them. Dead pause.)* Andy?

ANDY. *(Holds up his plate.)* This is our galaxy. Earth and our solar system are about here. *(Marks a spot out toward the edge.)* This is really very beautiful. And — Mickey? *(Mickey holds up a plate, some distance from Andy's.)*

MICKEY. Andromeda.

ANDY. That's the other large galaxy in our group, Andromeda. And — *(Holds up Sue's plate, she takes it.)* — that's the galaxy Cygnas Five. A little more on its side, Sue. Good. And Liz? *(She holds up a plate.)* And they're about twenty others. Professor? *(Carl holds up his plate close to Andy's Milky Way.)*

CARL. Make this one of the Magellanic Clouds. And Barbara, Pauly, Father. Good — To represent some of the others. *(They hold up their plates.)*

ANDY. Good. And each galaxy is spinning. *(He begins turning his plate, using both hands, on it's "axis." Then they all do.)* Great. And as Professor White was trying to point out, all the galaxies in our group are turning around a common center. So it's — everyone walk to his right. *(They do, slowly, "rotating" their plates with their two hands as they walk around the table.)* And this is our Local Galaxy Group! *(Pauly hums loudly something like the theme from* Star Wars.* *Mickey steps out of the turning group, looking at them.)*

MICKEY. Are we going to order any time soon? *(They stop in confusion and look at him. After a confused beat, they find their places and sit.)*

CARL. I'm afraid I have to make my apologies. I'll see you Monday. Ladies and gentlemen, it's been a pleasure. Andy, if you hear nothing from the president, call in the telegram first thing in the morning. 5 A.M.

MICKEY. All right!

ANDY. Say it so everyone at the bar can hear it, Carl.

CARL. I thought I had. Think of me in snowy Denver. *(They protest lightly and watch him leave. A short pause.)*

PAULY. What a tedious man. There was no reason on earth for him to tell us that. He didn't know we already knew it.

---

* See Special Note on Songs and Recordings on copyright page.

DON. "The conference is Heads of Departments."
SUE. "I went to your show to scoff."
ANDY. He went to her show because the wife of the Dean of the college thinks Barbara's great, so Carl damn well better know her work.
DON. And like it.
MICKEY. He's just excited. We're used to him.
LIZ. No, I wouldn't advise getting used to Professor White.
DON. Professor White in the Observatory with a meat cleaver.
PAULY. And I love the British.
LIZ. Did anyone else think he was hitting on Pauly?
SUE. Definitely.
PAULY. Oh, god, that's all I need.
MICKEY. He's married and he has two kids.
LIZ. You are so — sweet.
MICKEY. What? That doesn't mean anything?
DON. No, Mickey, I'm afraid that doesn't mean anything.
PAULY. He wasn't coming on to me. I do still remember what that feels like.
DON. Now that he's gone, Andy, Mickey, congratulations. Here's to your whatever it is.
MICKEY. It doesn't mean anything that he's married and has kids?
ANDY. Hell, you guys were there. It's as much yours as ours.
SUE. Here's to *our* —
DON, SUE, ANDY, MICKEY and PAULY. To *our* whatever it is!
SUE. And Pauly on is Birthday.
PAULY. Touch glass, ring the bell. Drive the devil away. *(All stand. Liz and Barbara have said, "To your whatever it is." Barbara toasts with her water.)*
SUE. Barbara. Don't do that! It's bad luck to toast with water.
ANDY. You're not drinking?
BARBARA. God, no. I'm not actually very hungry either. *(This conversation overlaps the continuing dialogue of Andy and Barbara.)*
PAULY. Just so there's no confusion, the "whatever it is" they've found is a huge object where the realization of the laws of physics is completely different from everything we know.

DON.   I think we knew that.

LIZ.   We did?

SUE.   Yeah, we did.

MICKEY.   *Maybe* different.

ANDY.   You sick again?

BARBARA.   I'm not in the absolutely best shape. No, I'm fine.

LIZ.   You shouldn't have come.

BARBARA.   I shouldn't have tried to work this afternoon.

ANDY.   How come?

BARBARA.   What?

DON.   *(Opening his menu.)* Let's get serious here.

ANDY.   Where's it hurt?

BARBARA.   It's Friday, Andy. Wake up. Nothing. Later.

ANDY.   So? I mean — And? What?

LIZ.   She said not now, Andy.

SUE.   I think I know what I want.

ANDY.   No wait. What?

BARBARA.   Later!

ANDY.   *(Having difficulty breathing.)* Oh. Right. Right.

DON.   *(To Liz.)* You want me to read that or can you make it out?

SUE.   *(To Mickey.)* You decided?

MICKEY.   I always have the same thing.

ANDY.   *(Has doubled over as though struck.)* Oh, god.

PAULY.   What?

ANDY.   I can't breathe.

PAULY.   Put your head down.

ANDY.   I'm not breathing.

DON.   Slap him on the back.

ANDY.   Jesus, Barbara! What did you...? No. No. God! Oh!

BARBARA.   What?

ANDY.   *What?* You can say what? Oh, god.

BARBARA.   Could you not be so fucking self-dramatizing for once? *(Getting up.)* Mom's right, I feel like hell. Pauly, I'm sorry —

ANDY.   No! You're not leaving.

LIZ.   *(An alert.)* Don.

BARBARA.   *(To Andy.)* We'll talk later.

ANDY.   There's nothing to say. What's left to talk about. You saw to that —

BARBARA.   *(Turning to go.)* Well, it's time to leave. —

ANDY.   You willful — bitch! *(Andy steps in front of her exit and slaps her, she immediately slaps him back.)*

BARBARA.   You fuck! What the hell do you think —

MICKEY.   Hey, what are you doing, Andy?

SUE.   *(Simultaneous.)* Oh, my god.

ANDY.   You willful bitch. *(Andy slugs Barbara, shockingly hard. She staggers back, falls to the floor, and before Don or Mickey can get up from the table and get to him, he has kicked her several times, repeating "bitch, bitch!" Mickey has turned his chair over, Sue screams as Andy kicks Barbara.)*

DON.   Stop it! *(Don and Mickey grab Andy, dragging him away from Barbara.)*

ANDY.   Get off me, goddamnit.

LIZ.   Leave her alone.

ANDY.   You murdering bitch! *(Andy tries to get away from the men, struggling toward Barbara.)*

DON.   Andy, stop it. What the hell's wrong with you?

ANDY.   Let go. *(He stops struggling.)* I don't hit people. I've never hit anyone in my life, I don't know — Yes! Bleed, bitch!

DON.   *(As Andy tries to pull away again.)* I'll knock your damn heart out, I'm not kidding.

ANDY.   What heart? What heart? She did that already.

LIZ.   *(To Barbara.)* Don't try to get up.

DON.   Get out. Get out of here.

ANDY.   *(To Barbara.)* Did I — I can't — I'll be OK, give me —

DON.   Andy, leave. Go on, get out.

PAULY.   Get out of here, asshole. I'll call the cops. Out. Leave. *(Andy storms out. Don yells after him.)*

DON.   I'm not kidding, stay away from her…. *(To Mickey.)* See that he doesn't come back in here. *(To Barbara as Mickey runs off.)* Dear God. Don't try to get up. Lie still. *(She gets up with a bleeding lip and forehead.)*

PAULY.   Oh, god above. *(Sue has gone to the bar, she brings a damp towel, hands it to Liz who hands it to Don.)*

BARBARA.   *(She spits out her words with difficulty.)* Am I —

bleeding?

LIZ.   What are you talking about, of course you're bleeding.

BARBARA.   *(Holding her side.)* Good. Good.

DON.   Sit down. *(She sits at a table. He and Liz sit with her. Pauly stands by the table. Mickey comes back.)*

MICKEY.   He's gone.

DON.   What the hell is going on here?

BARBARA.   A little domes — tic friction!

PAULY.   I'm going to call a doctor.

BARBARA.   For what? A house call?

LIZ.   Ha! Fat chance.

DON.   You can be funny? He'd have killed you!

BARBARA.   Tit for fucking Tat!

LIZ.   Bullfeathers.

DON.   This is something that happens all the time? This is what your relationship is based on? Do you get to beat him up in public next time? What the hell is this? Jesus, your head's cut.

BARBARA.   Stop — cluck — ing. I'm Okay.

DON.   Clucking is the thing I do best.

SUE.   I think he was drunk when he got here.

BARBARA.   I'm a beer battered woman.

MICKEY.   Who's he talking about murdering? I've never seen him like that.

SUE.   I've never seen anyone like that.

PAULY.   *(Realizing what's up.)* Oh, god. Oh, no. Oh, Barbara.

BARBARA.   *(She has been trying to speak.)* Don.

DON.   What? What?

BARBARA.   Could you — take me to — the hospital? I think I have a — broken rib. *(Pauly is sitting at the end of the table, his face in his hands, crying his eyes out.)*

PAULY.   Oh, no. Oh, honey. Oh, why? Oh, god.

DON.   Pauly, straighten up, now's not the time for that. Do you have your car here?

PAULY.   *(Still crying.)* Oh, god. Yeah, sure. I'll get it. *(Everybody leaves except Mickey and Sue. Both are shaken.)*

SUE.   Oh, brother.

MICKEY.   Can you tell me what the hell...?

SUE.   What's the word you used? I guess that was an example of non-linear behavior.

MICKEY.   Yeah, that was definitely "going non-linear." What the hell ticked him off? I mean he was mad anyway.

SUE.   She had an abortion Mickey, wake-up.

MICKEY.   Today? And then goes out after something like that? Can you do that?

SUE.   Apparently not. I'm sorry. I didn't know what was going on till Pauly started bawling. Oh, god.

MICKEY.   Are you all right?

SUE.   No. I'm not all right. I want a lot of children. Do you want a lot of children?

MICKEY.   You kidding? I'm Italian. Ten or fifteen.

SUE.   That sounds about right.

PAULY.   *(Off.)* I just keep thinking "Violence! Violence!"

MICKEY.   You want to go?

SUE.   Let's finish the wine. Also I don't think I could walk.

(Pauly's house. Barbara, Liz and Pauly have walked in over the above scene. Barbara sits. Liz is standing by, thoughtful. Barbara's forehead is bandaged, an arm is in a sling. Pauly is all over the place, a nervous wreck, clearing everything from the table, unexpected guests, rattling on.)

PAULY.   What's that from? A little old lady running around screaming, "Violence!" It's so prevalent in our society — you just don't expect to see it in your own — as they always say.

BARBARA.   *Baby Doll.*

PAULY.   I know, I'm blathering, I'm no good to you at all. What do you need?

BARBARA.   "Violence! Violence!" It's from the movie, *Baby Doll.*

PAULY.   *(Still rattling on.)* Oh. Well…. No. You're right, but I was thinking…. Oh, god. Sandy Dennis in *Who's Afraid of Virginia Woolf?.* Peeling the labels off brandy bottles, watching everyone beat everyone up and yelling, "Violence! Violence!" It's almost her entire part. Maybe Albee was quoting *Baby Doll.* To hell with it. It's a violent society. It's a violent cosmos. Every element on Earth, including everything in us, comes from some star that exploded billions of years — why shouldn't our atoms be inherently unstable. Borne from violence, can't help

60

but be violent. We shouldn't be surprised that we're crazy.

BARBARA. Pauly.

PAULY. I know. I'm rattling. Don't talk if it hurts.

BARBARA. It doesn't hurt. I'm laced with pain killers. They gave me some kind of — I didn't know what they were doing or I'd have told them to get the hell off me.

PAULY. *(Suddenly very interested.)* Laced with exactly what manner of pain killers?

BARBARA. You're incorrigible. They gave Don the prescriptions, he had them filled. *(She hands her purse to Pauly who searches through it, finding a bag from the pharmacy.)*

PAULY. We live in the age of chemistry, Barbara. Drug companies spend a fortune harassing us with the horrors of death and pain so they can push these little palliatives on us. *(He puts on his reading glasses.)* We pay enormous mark-ups to foster an oppressive class system that grinds two thirds of its people into the dirt, where what do we do to alleviate our pain? We take drugs, Barbara.

BARBARA. I know.

PAULY. That's why artists find it difficult to earn the public's trust. You don't play along.

BARBARA. And you guys are giving San Francisco a great reputation.

PAULY. Everyone says. "Those damned Chorus Masters." *(Looking at the label of one.)* Whoa. You're right, this is no good for you. *(Pockets it, looks at the other.)* Percodan? Lord above, the mother lode. No disparagement intended. To either of you.

BARBARA. Fuck yourself.

PAULY. Well, someone should.

BARBARA. Are you still pining after Don?

PAULY. *(Bitchy.)* Would you like some tea? Or maybe you just want to rest your mouth.

BARBARA. *(Laughs, but it hurts.)* Ouch. Damn. Good idea. I should probably lie down for real. Are you going out?

PAULY. Of course not, I don't go out.

BARBARA. I'm okay here.

PAULY. As you said, I have my love. If you want something you have to *Call My Name.* Generic screams of agony, gun shots, living in this neighborhood, I sleep right through them. *(Liz has been lost in her own thoughts. Now, recalling something that's been bothering her. Almost to herself, but it stops everyone.)*

LIZ. Sympathetic magic.

PAULY. How's that, darling?

LIZ. I was trying to remember what Frazer called it. In *The Golden Bough*. The rituals one performs to cause what one wants to happen. Like lighting a great bonfire, believing it will cause the sun to shine. Sympathetic magic. It's a superstition ritual. Villagers in Africa still practice it. If they want the rains to come, they make the sound of rain. Pretend it's raining. "Pat-pat-pat-pat-pat-pat-pat."

BARBARA. That was the sound of rain?

LIZ. On a broad-leaved ficus, I was thinking. *Ficus elastica* wouldn't be stretching it, would it?

PAULY. And does it work?

LIZ. Well, it must work from time to time or the silly bastards wouldn't still be doing it.

BARBARA. Your point being: *(A distant car horn is heard.)*

LIZ. That's my cab. My point being: Magic doesn't prepare us for these little speed bumps of real life. *They* pretend it's raining, act out rain, believing it will cause it to rain. And *we* act out good partnerships, or marriages, families, *life* — believing it will cause a real partnership or a worthwhile life to happen. Same thing.

BARBARA. Yeah. Well, good "luck."

LIZ. We shouldn't expect it. That's not life, that's voodoo. I'll be over in the morning.

ANDY. *(Off.)* I've never hit anyone before in my life.

BARBARA. It's not necessary, really.

LIZ. I know you'd rather have Pauly, but he's got practice. *(Barbara goes off one way, to the bedroom, Liz the other. Pauly stands in the room a moment longer. Don and Andy enter, at the Warehouse/Studio. Don is packing a few things for Barbara in an overnight bag.)*

ANDY. Really, I'm not like that. That wasn't me.

DON. I hear that a lot.

ANDY. Yeah?

DON. The devil made me do it. She has two cracked ribs, a dislocated shoulder, a gash on her head and multiple "contusions." Which turns out to mean "bruises." I had to ask.

ANDY. Oh, man.

DON. No internal damage. There could have been. Her body was already traumatized.

ANDY. I know. I know that. Traumatized! Shit! *(Beat.)* I've never been angry like that. I just snapped. Every measure of feeling I had for her evaporated in a second.

DON. Are you pleading temporary insanity?

ANDY. I don't know. It might be permanent. Yes. I wanted to kill her. Haven't you ever hit anyone?

DON. I was usually bigger than they were.

ANDY. Tell me about it. "No internal damages." The internal damage she'd already had done to herself. What's your progressive opinion on that one, Father?

DON. I have no solace for you. What are you feeling now?

ANDY. I feel exactly the same as I did the second I knew what she'd done. I feel sick. To my stomach. I feel betrayed on the most basic sexual — I want none of it to have happened. Or. Maybe I think there's got to be some way to get back to —

DON. Don't beat yourself up, I won't believe it. If you weren't so lost in the stars, you'd at least have remembered what day it was.

ANDY. I know that. The work happens to be goddamn important. Also I spent two hours in the ER. Look at this contraption. *(He opens his shirt. His chest and shoulder are bound. Very distantly we begin to hear Mozart's* Requiem. *)*

DON. What the hell's that?

ANDY. You broke my fucking collar bone.

DON. I did that? Good. I mean I'm terribly sorry. At least you can work. Barbara won't be able to work for a month.

ANDY. Most of my work is done in my head.

DON. I should have given you a concussion.

ANDY. I thought you two didn't get along.

DON. She's my sister, asshole.

* See Special Note on Songs and Recordings on copyright page.

ANDY. *(Getting up.)* Ouch! I have to get back to work, Don. Or go to bed, I haven't slept in three days — nights.

DON. You coming any closer to quantifying God?

ANDY. That's not in my project description. Unless He's utterly unexpected and unfathomable.

DON. I'd think He would be.

ANDY. Why not, throwing jokers in the deck. Well, without more massive atom smashers, we're taking a lot on blind faith, just like you.

DON. *"Blind* faith" is redundant. Faith is blind. All this "Give me a sign, God, to prove You exist" is blasphemy.

ANDY. Well, you follow your faith, I'll follow mine. Probably we're not that far apart.

DON. Don't think that. We're light years apart. Barbara asked if you could be out by tomorrow night. *(Don leaves with the overnight bag. The* Requiem* *soars for a moment. Pauly and Liz walk into the church garden, listening. Pauly is smoking, Liz is wearing lightly tinted sunglasses. The* Requiem* *continues under the scene.)*

PAULY. That sounds great from out here. Maybe we should bring the congregation out to the courtyard. Or I should conduct from out here. Mozart, Liz. Isn't that the ridiculous cliché? Aren't we always saying they could be the next Mozart? Or could have been the next Mozart?

LIZ. When did you take up smoking?

PAULY. I've always smoked. Just not much. One a day. *(Re the music.)* This is tricky, they'll fuck it up. *(Listens.)* No. Not bad.

LIZ. It's beautiful.

PAULY. Written on his deathbed, we're led to believe, and unfinished. Just for you and yours. Are those new glasses?

LIZ. No. I just haven't been wearing them. The light — it's too damn sunny here. I need to move to Seattle.

PAULY. Everybody says that.

LIZ. Who's conducting?

PAULY. My assistant. Nice lesbian. I always mention that or people assume I have some sweet-cheeked young boy protégé.

* See Special Note on Songs and Recordings on copyright page.

They never take their eyes off the score anyway. You look impatient. Or you look more impatient than usual.

LIZ.   Nothing, it's fine. Stomach.

PAULY.   Liz, it's obviously damned serious. It scares me to think you're down there with the gangs and can't see what the hell they're up to.

LIZ.   I finished that.

PAULY.   Finished? Really? You're done?

LIZ.   It wasn't working. I don't know if you can observe a group without effecting their behavior.

PAULY.   You're observing your effect on the group. Heisenberg's Uncertainty Principle. *(Liz is shading her eyes with her hand.)* Can you see me at all?

LIZ.   Of course I can see you. It's not that bad.

PAULY.   Bullfeathers. You're blind as a bat and sick to your stomach.

LIZ.   I'm sick from the medication more than anything.

PAULY.   Fuck. I'd rather have whatever the medication is supposed to be curing than be sick. Don't you — *(It dawns on him.)* Oh, good lord, Liz.

LIZ.   *(Annoyed.)* What?

PAULY.   How?

LIZ.   Pauly, don't be enigmatic. I'm impatient as it is.

PAULY.   I was going to say how would you get it, but that's easy. I've been incredibly obtuse. Anyone who spent that much time in Zaire.

LIZ.   Certainly not. Not anyone, Pauly. Shame on you. Anyone who took a doctor for a lover, if that doctor happened to have a former wife who was dying. What did we know back then? We didn't even know it was sexually transmitted. It's not worth talking about.

PAULY.   Oh, Christ. What are they doing for you? What's your medication?

LIZ.   Pauly, shut up about it. They've tried every cocktail combination — I'm at the point I'd much rather settle for vodka.

PAULY.   I have friends who didn't respond for months, then their T cells just — they'll find something that works.

LIZ.   I'll tell you right now, I don't sing. So forget about it.

Also, I wouldn't be able to read the damn score. I would almost try to sing if I thought I could make something that beautiful. *(The Chorus stops.)* What happened?

PAULY. You've suddenly gone deaf. That's the end of the section we're working on.

LIZ. Do me the favor of not mentioning it.

PAULY. Sure. Don knows?

LIZ. I've told him I expect his hospice to be ready by the time I need it. *(Pauly starts to approach her.)* Oh, get away! Go lead your band.

PAULY. Take care of yourself. *(Liz starts to leave, seems uncertain of her footing. She calls.)*

LIZ. Pauly! *(He goes to her.)* Give me your hand. This sun is fucking agony. *(Andy's office. Mickey and Andy are both furious, Mickey is reading a newspaper. Carl enters. They are leading him on, so what they say is not what they mean.)*

CARL. Good, you're both here.

MICKEY. How was Denver?

CARL. I've organized a meeting, here, three weeks from today. I think we can expect the most stellar constellation of scientists every assembled in this state. You may disagree with my methods, but I've decided to open our problem up to —

ANDY. — Carl, Mickey and I have been in this office for the last hour answering the phone and saying, No Comment.

CARL. Good, that's exactly right.

MICKEY. I've hung up twice on Goddard Space Flight Center.

CARL. You knew they'd bite on this.

ANDY. How could you have been that stupid? Even you. *(Carl is stunned. He turns to leave.)* Don't you dare leave this room!

CARL. You have only your personal reputation to enhance. Which, I must say, up till now you've done extraordinarily well. I have to think about the advantage to the school.

ANDY. I'm glad you brought up personal reputations. Where's the front page, Mickey? You can't tell us you haven't seen this.

MICKEY. *(Reading the paper.)* "White Ratio Baffles Physicists!"

ANDY. White Ratio. That nicely balances Brown Dwarfs and Red Giants and Black Holes.

CARL. *(Looking at the paper.)* Well, that's unfortunate. That can be addressed. That's some headline writer's idea of a pun.

ANDY. Carl you read the paper every morning.

CARL. *(Firmly.)* I had not seen that paper. That's unfortunate. It's a small thing. It can be addressed.

MICKEY. *(Reading.)* "San Francisco Astrophysicist Carl Conklin *White* astonished a group of scientists on the *first day* of a weekend conference in Denver with the announcement that a team from his Observatory —"

ANDY. — No names, just The A Team —

MICKEY. — That's OK, fuck it — "had discovered an object in the far distant past of the universe that all of science tells us can not exist."

CARL. The *Chronicle* got it completely wrong.

ANDY. — We don't have three weeks. Every scientist in the world is going to be looking for the answer to this. And they'll find it.

MICKEY. *(Reading.)* — "Said this brings into question several assumptions of quantum theory ..."

CARL. Are you in this too, Picco? That surprises me.

MICKEY. In what?

CARL. I *intend* for every scientist in the world to come here and present his findings. From here. If this discovery helps clear up what I think are some very rough spots in quantum mechanics, the cameras will have focused on this school.

ANDY. And you will have looked like a fossil. A big fossil of an asshole with a label on it that says Carl Conklin White's Ratio.

CARL. Dr. Anderson, you are walking on very unsure ground. I don't believe I've ever been so shocked or angry as I am at this moment. This university can tolerate a great many things but negligence is not among them.

ANDY. Well, you've lost me.

CARL. I arrived at my hotel in Denver at 8 in the morning. 7 California time. I unpacked my bags, called down for breakfast, and rang up John Malloy at the Astronomy Society. Well, what do you think, I said. About what? About the discovery my boys have made. Mickey Picco and Andy Anderson. Oh, I think you're mistaken, he says. I've had no call from Andy. I scramble and fumble for my notes. Thank god I'd brought them with me. I had every right not to mention the two of you at all. The discovery was recorded as made by the four of us. Against my better judgment. I *had* to put my name on it, damnit. I called in the telegram!

MICKEY.   Four of us?

ANDY.   Farnov.

MICKEY.   Right, of course.

CARL.   And yes, I asked to be the first speaker of the morning, just to say a few words. Every astronomer in the room would have it on his e-mail within the hour. Did you oversleep, did it slip your mind, did you — what?

ANDY.   I passed out.

CARL.   I know all about it. Beating up your live-in girlfriend in a restaurant filled with scientists from every school in the county. The two of you spending half the night in separate hospitals. And you have the insolence to lecture me on ethics. I get a call from Malloy the next morning. Well, your boy finally called in. A day late and a dollar short. It was in the papers by then. It's amazing they mentioned the school at all. *(Collects himself.)* I've asked that you be relieved from your teaching assignments. You'll need to devote your time to this seminar. I'll assign someone else to the next lecture series.

ANDY.   Carl —

CARL.   I don't want to hear anything from you. I want to hear nothing from you. *(Carl turns and leaves. Andy starts after him.)*

ANDY.   I need that series, Carl. Carl! Damn him.

MICKEY.   Jellybeans from a baby.

ANDY.   That's our discovery. Yours. It's your discovery. I'm sorry, Mickey.

MICKEY.   "The Mickey Picco Ratio" doesn't have the same ring to it. You went to the hospital?

ANDY.   You and that Queer Giant Priest friend of yours broke my clavicle. And of course Carl's spies told him all about it. They couldn't wait. I think I'm dying. My shoulder is killing me. *(Mickey is grinning.)* What? My head is throbbing like a turbine — Oh, man. — *What?*

MICKEY. I'm in love. *(Mickey walks out, Andy is standing in the middle of the Warehouse/Studio. Barbara is at a table, sketching on a huge pad. Her left arm is in a sling.)*
ANDY. This is very difficult.
BARBARA. Just don't apologize. It hurts when I laugh.
ANDY. Yeah. How are your —
BARBARA. The shoulder is getting better, it constricts my movement but not that much. Fortunately it was the left side. The discomfort is in the damn ribs. When I — *(Breathes deeply.)* Aye! It hurts like hell when I take a deep breath.
ANDY. Ouch! Don't —
BARBARA. I know. Don't do that.
ANDY. Yeah. *(Very pained.)* I — uh —
BARBARA. Oh, please. No, what?
ANDY. I really did love you.
BARBARA. Yeah, well — we both had a funny way of showing it.
ANDY. I'm kind of lost here.
BARBARA. *(With more energy.)* You've always thought *I* was fanatical: intense, focused, consumed with my work. But you have got to meet the Ambulance-Chasing Battered Woman Legal Aide Banshee at the hospital. Now there's a woman with fire in her belly. Badgering me to press charges against you. It was a pretty attractive idea for a minute or two.
ANDY. You probably should have.
BARBARA. Gal actually said, "Let me run with this, I can complete destroy the bastard's life." You got the feeling most of the men she deals with don't have a life worth destroying. At the very least she wanted me to get an order of protection.
ANDY. You didn't get an —
BARBARA. No, of course not. But she made me think. Sad, doe-eyed, the picture of broken hope when she was leaving, I mean this girl was an *actress*. She turned and said, "You're going to go back to him, aren't you?" Wow. I hadn't even thought. You live with someone, share whatever you can share — did I want to come back to this studio barn by myself?
ANDY. What did you say?
BARBARA. I said, "Check back with me on that one." Then I

said, "No. I'd like to try living alone."

ANDY.   Yeah. I really am — so profoundly sorry.

BARBARA.   *(Laughs, holds her side.)* Oh, you bastard. I told you not to say that. Mom said we don't live our life, we live some fiction. Voodoo. I want to try to live my — Oh, Christ, I sound like every New Age flake in California.

ANDY.   Will you be able to afford this place alone?

BARBARA.   It looks like it.

ANDY.   You're not going to be teaching next semester.

BARBARA.   No, probably I will.

ANDY.   Well, I probably won't. Not here. I have my last lecture of the series and that's it.

BARBARA.   Running away? That doesn't sound like you.

ANDY.   What I need to do can't be done here anymore. I'm writing a paper with Mickey for Carl's conference a couple of weeks from now. Mickey's going to deliver it. He's scared to death. *(She just stares at him.)* — Well —

BARBARA.   Yeah. I can't think of another word that hasn't been said.

ANDY.   I know. Well. I'll see you around.

BARBARA.   And around and around and around. *(Barbara removes the sling, stretches her arms high in freedom. Andy turns to look back to Barbara and Don in the church garden.)*

DON.   I've always liked this courtyard.

BARBARA.   It's huge.

DON.   We're going to knock windows in the hospice. So the school and the hospice will both look out on the lawn. We use it for receptions when the weather's good. You don't know Mrs. Melon. She considers it her mission to glorify the city with her superb taste. She's offered the Church a work of art. I tried to get her to donate to the Hospice Fund but that isn't her style. I sent her to your gallery. She fell in love with the big steel piece, so she actually does have taste.

BARBARA.   *Flight.* It's called.

DON.   Flight? I guess I could make it look aeronautical if I thought about —

BARBARA.   Flight of spirit, flight of fancy. Flight of time.

DON.   She wants to meet you. Apparently a Minneapolis museum is taking one of your pieces from the show.

BARBARA.   The Walker.

DON.   Mrs. Melon says they're considered an arbiter of taste or something. If they take a piece, several other museums will follow suit. They're a kind of confidence decoy.

BARBARA.   I don't know what that is.

DON.   You've seen the big white swan decoys? They're called confidence decoys. Hunters use them on ducks. Swans won't swim somewhere that's dangerous. So a confidence decoy makes the ducks believe the lake is safe.

BARBARA.   That's diabolical.

DON.   I've always thought there was a metaphor there somewhere. Anyway, we're going to put your piece in the center of the court here. I wanted you to see the space. I don't know if there should be paving under it, as a base, or just set it directly on the grass.

BARBARA.   *(Suddenly understanding.)* Wait!

DON.   *(Beat.)* I thought you'd like the idea.

BARBARA.   *(Breathless.)* I've always thought of my work as pretty secular.

DON.   No work of art is secular. Art praises God. Or humankind. Same thing. *(Barbara, with tears in her eyes, walks around the spot, checking it out.)* It'll really look good here.

BARBARA.   Yes, it will.

DON.   Mrs. Melon says we have to move fast. After the news about Minneapolis leeks, the whole show will sell out.

BARBARA.   I know.

DON.   She thinks at least one piece from your first show should stay in San Francisco. *(Pause.)* You're very good. You deserve the success.

BARBARA.   *(Crying.)* No base. Directly on the grass. *(Don leaves. Barbara continues to sit in the courtyard, looking at the space. Andy turns back to the audience.)*

ANDY.   Looking far back in time, science tells us, the laws of physics should be about the same as they are now. And until now all our observations have confirmed that. We have no ex-

71

planation for the anomaly we've found.

Like those unpredictable subatomic particles of which we're made, unexpected events throw our understanding of the universe into chaos.

It's the mystery that's reality. Not the theories we construct to explain the unknown.

Now, why, you will ask me, have I chosen to speak on the universe, rather than some other topic.

Well, it's very simple. There isn't anything else.

END OF PLAY

PROPERTY LIST

Folded sheet of paper (ANDY)
Glasses of red wine (DON, SUE, MICKEY)
Towel (ANDY)
3 tall drinks (BARBARA, LIZ, SUE)
2 beers (ANDY)
Plate (CARL)
Carafe of red wine
Martini (PAULY)
Whiskey (ANDY)
Carafe of wine (ANDY)
Dinner plates (ANDY, MICKEY, SUE, LIZ, CARL,
        BARBARA, PAULY, DON)
Menu (DON)
Damp towel
Purse (BARBARA) with pharmacy bag with pills
Reading glasses (PAULY)
Overnight bag (DON)
Personal items for Barbara (DON)
Cigarette, lit (PAULY)
Tinted sunglasses (LIZ)
Sling (BARBARA)
Sketch pad (BARBARA)

SOUND EFFECTS

Elevator
Console beep
Distant car horn

NEW PLAYS

★ **HONOUR by Joanna Murray-Smith.** In a series of intense confrontations, a wife, husband, lover and daughter negotiate the forces of passion, history, responsibility and honour. "HONOUR makes for surprisingly interesting viewing. Tight, crackling dialogue (usually played out in punchy verbal duels) captures characters unable to deal with emotions ... Murray-Smith effectively places her characters in situations that strip away pretense." *–Variety* "... the play's virtues are strong: a distinctive theatrical voice, passionate concerns ... HONOUR might just capture a few honors of its own." *–Time Out Magazine* [1M, 3W] ISBN: 0-8222-1683-3

★ **MR. PETERS' CONNECTIONS by Arthur Miller.** Mr. Miller describes the protagonist as existing in a dream-like state when the mind is "freed to roam from real memories to conjectures, from trivialities to tragic insights, from terror of death to glorying in one's being alive." With this memory play, the Tony Award and Pulitzer Prize-winner reaffirms his stature as the world's foremost dramatist. "... a cross between Joycean stream-of-consciousness and Strindberg's dream plays, sweetened with a dose of William Saroyan's philosophical whimsy ... CONNECTIONS is most intriguing ..." *–The NY Times* [5M, 3W] ISBN: 0-8222-1687-6

★ **THE WAITING ROOM by Lisa Loomer.** Three women from different centuries meet in a doctor's waiting room in this dark comedy about the timeless quest for beauty – and its cost. "... THE WAITING ROOM ... is a bold, risky melange of conflicting elements that is ... terrifically moving ... There's no resisting the fierce emotional pull of the play." *–The NY Times* "... one of the high points of this year's Off-Broadway season ... THE WAITING ROOM is well worth a visit." *–Back Stage* [7M, 4W, flexible casting] ISBN: 0-8222-1594-2

★ **THE OLD SETTLER by John Henry Redwood.** A sweet-natured comedy about two church-going sisters in 1943 Harlem and the handsome young man who rents a room in their apartment. "For all of its decent sentiments, THE OLD SETTLER avoids sentimentality. It has the authenticity and lack of pretense of an Early American sampler." *–The NY Times* "We've had some fine plays Off-Broadway this season, and this is one of the best." *–The NY Post* [1M, 3W] ISBN: 0-8-222-1642-6

★ **LAST TRAIN TO NIBROC by Arlene Hutton.** In 1940 two young strangers share a seat on a train bound east only to find their paths will cross again. "All aboard. LAST TRAIN TO NIBROC is a sweetly told little chamber romance." *–Show Business* "... [a] gently charming little play, reminiscent of Thornton Wilder in its look at rustic Americans who are to be treasured for their simplicity and directness ..." *–Associated Press* "The old formula of boy wins girls, boy loses girl, boy wins girl still works ... [a] well-made play that perfectly captures a slice of small-town-life-gone-by." *–Back Stage* [1M, 1W] ISBN: 0-8222-1753-8

★ **OVER THE RIVER AND THROUGH THE WOODS by Joe DiPietro.** Nick sees both sets of his grandparents every Sunday for dinner. This is routine until he has to tell them that he's been offered a dream job in Seattle. The news doesn't sit so well. "A hilarious family comedy that is even funnier than his long running musical revue *I Love You, You're Perfect, Now Change.*" *–Back Stage* "Loaded with laughs every step of the way." *–Star-Ledger* [3M, 3W] ISBN: 0-8222-1712-0

★ **SIDE MAN by Warren Leight.** 1999 Tony Award winner. This is the story of a broken family and the decline of jazz as popular entertainment. "... a tender, deeply personal memory play about the turmoil in the family of a jazz musician as his career crumbles at the dawn of the age of rock-and-roll ..." *–The NY Times* "[SIDE MAN] is an elegy for two things – a lost world and a lost love. When the two notes sound together in harmony, it is moving and graceful ..." *–The NY Daily News* "An atmospheric memory play ... with crisp dialogue and clearly drawn characters ... reflects the passing of an era with persuasive insight ... The joy and despair of the musicians is skillfully illustrated." *–Variety* [5M, 3W] ISBN: 0-8222-1721-X

DRAMATISTS PLAY SERVICE, INC.
440 Park Avenue South, New York, NY 10016 212-683-8960 Fax 212-213-1539
postmaster@dramatists.com   www.dramatists.com

NEW PLAYS

★ **CLOSER by Patrick Marber.** Winner of the 1998 Olivier Award for Best Play and the 1999 New York Drama Critics Circle Award for Best Foreign Play. Four lives intertwine over the course of four and a half years in this densely plotted, stinging look at modern love and betrayal. "CLOSER is a sad, savvy, often funny play that casts a steely, unblinking gaze at the world of relationships and lets you come to your own conclusions … CLOSER does not merely hold your attention; it burrows into you." –*New York Magazine* "A powerful, darkly funny play about the cosmic collision between the sun of love and the comet of desire." –*Newsweek Magazine* [2M, 2W] ISBN: 0-8222-1722-8

★ **THE MOST FABULOUS STORY EVER TOLD by Paul Rudnick.** A stage manager, headset and prompt book at hand, brings the house lights to half, then dark, and cues the creation of the world. Throughout the play, she's in control of everything. In other words, she's either God, or she thinks she is. "Line by line, Mr. Rudnick may be the funniest writer for the stage in the United States today … One-liners, epigrams, withering put-downs and flashing repartee: These are the candles that Mr. Rudnick lights instead of cursing the darkness … a testament to the virtues of laughing … and in laughter, there is something like the memory of Eden." –*The NY Times* "Funny it is … consistently, rapaciously, deliriously … easily the funniest play in town." –*Variety* [4M, 5W] ISBN: 0-8222-1720-1

★ **A DOLL'S HOUSE by Henrik Ibsen, adapted by Frank McGuinness.** Winner of the 1997 Tony Award for Best Revival. "New, raw, gut-twisting and gripping. Easily the hottest drama this season." –*USA Today* "Bold, brilliant and alive." –*The Wall Street Journal* "A thunderclap of an evening that takes your breath away." –*Time Magazine* [4M, 4W, 2 boys] ISBN: 0-8222-1636-1

★ **THE HERBAL BED by Peter Whelan.** The play is based on actual events which occurred in Stratford-upon-Avon in the summer of 1613, when William Shakespeare's elder daughter was publicly accused of having a sexual liaison with a married neighbor and family friend. "In his probing new play, THE HERBAL BED … Peter Whelan muses about a sidelong event in the life of Shakespeare's family and creates a finely textured tapestry of love and lies in the early 17th-century Stratford." –*The NY Times* "It is a first rate drama with interesting moral issues of truth and expediency." –*The NY Post* [5M, 3W] ISBN: 0-8222-1675-2

★ **SNAKEBIT by David Marshall Grant.** A study of modern friendship when put to the test. "… a rather smart and absorbing evening of water-cooler theater, the intimate sort of Off-Broadway experience that has you picking apart the recognizable characters long after the curtain calls." – *The NY Times* "Off-Broadway keeps on presenting us with compelling reasons for going to the theater. The latest is SNAKEBIT, David Marshall Grant's smart new comic drama about being thirtysomething and losing one's way in life." –*The NY Daily News* [3M, 1W] ISBN: 0-8222-1724-4

★ **A QUESTION OF MERCY by David Rabe.** The Obie Award-winning playwright probes the sensitive and controversial issue of doctor-assisted suicide in the age of AIDS in this poignant drama. "There are many devastating ironies in Mr. Rabe's beautifully considered, piercingly clear-eyed work …" –*The NY Times* "With unsettling candor and disturbing insight, the play arouses pity and understanding of a troubling subject … Rabe's provocative tale is an affirmation of dignity that rings clear and true." –*Variety* [6M, 1W] ISBN: 0-8222-1643-4

★ **DIMLY PERCEIVED THREATS TO THE SYSTEM by Jon Klein.** Reality and fantasy overlap with hilarious results as this unforgettable family attempts to survive the nineties. "Here's a play whose point about fractured families goes to the heart, mind – and ears." –*The Washington Post* "… an end-of-the millennium comedy about a family on the verge of a nervous breakdown … Trenchant and hilarious …" –*The Baltimore Sun* [2M, 4W] ISBN: 0-8222-1677-9

DRAMATISTS PLAY SERVICE, INC.
440 Park Avenue South, New York, NY 10016 212-683-8960 Fax 212-213-1539
postmaster@dramatists.com www.dramatists.com

NEW PLAYS

★ **AS BEES IN HONEY DROWN by Douglas Carter Beane.** Winner of the John Gassner Playwriting Award. A hot young novelist finds the subject of his new screenplay in a New York socialite who leads him into the world of *Auntie Mame* and *Breakfast at Tiffany's*, before she takes him for a ride. "A delicious soufflé of a satire ... [an] extremely entertaining fable for an age that always chooses image over substance." *–The NY Times* "... A witty assessment of one of the most active and relentless industries in a consumer society ... the creation of 'hot' young things, which the media have learned to mass produce with efficiency and zeal." *–The NY Daily News* [3M, 3W, flexible casting] ISBN: 0-8222-1651-5

★ **STUPID KIDS by John C. Russell.** In rapid, highly stylized scenes, the story follows four high-school students as they make their way from first through eighth period and beyond, struggling with the fears, frustrations, and longings peculiar to youth. "In STUPID KIDS ... playwright John C. Russell gets the opera of adolescence to a T ... The stylized teenspeak of STUPID KIDS ... suggests that Mr. Russell may have hidden a tape recorder under a desk in study hall somewhere and then scoured the tapes for good quotations ... it is the kids' insular, ceaselessly churning world, a pre-adult world of Doritos and libidos, that the playwright seeks to lay bare." *–The NY Times* "STUPID KIDS [is] a sharp-edged ... whoosh of teen angst and conformity anguish. It is also very funny." *–NY Newsday* [2M, 2W] ISBN: 0-8222-1698-1

★ **COLLECTED STORIES by Donald Margulies.** From Obie Award-winner Donald Margulies comes a provocative analysis of a student-teacher relationship that turns sour when the protégé becomes a rival. "With his fine ear for detail, Margulies creates an authentic, insular world, and he gives equal weight to the opposing viewpoints of two formidable characters." *–The LA Times* "This is probably Margulies' best play to date ..." *–The NY Post* "... always fluid and lively, the play is thick with ideas, like a stock-pot of good stew." *–The Village Voice* [2W] ISBN: 0-8222-1640-X

★ **FREEDOMLAND by Amy Freed.** An overdue showdown between a son and his father sets off fireworks that illuminate the neurosis, rage and anxiety of one family – and of America at the turn of the millennium. "FREEDOMLAND's more obvious links are to *Buried Child* and *Bosoms and Neglect*. Freed, like Guare, is an inspired wordsmith with a gift for surreal touches in situations grounded in familiar and real territory." *–Curtain Up* [3M, 4W] ISBN: 0-8222-1719-8

★ **STOP KISS by Diana Son.** A poignant and funny play about the ways, both sudden and slow, that lives can change irrevocably. "There's so much that is vital and exciting about STOP KISS ... you want to embrace this young author and cheer her onto other works ... the writing on display here is funny and credible ... you also will be charmed by its heartfelt characters and up-to-the-minute humor." *–The NY Daily News* "... irresistibly exciting ... a sweet, sad, and enchantingly sincere play." *–The NY Times* [3M, 3W] ISBN: 0-8222-1731-7

★ **THREE DAYS OF RAIN by Richard Greenberg.** The sins of fathers and mothers make for a bittersweet elegy in this poignant and revealing drama. "... a work so perfectly judged it heralds the arrival of a major playwright ... Greenberg is extraordinary." *–The NY Daily News* "Greenberg's play is filled with graceful passages that are by turns melancholy, harrowing, and often, quite funny." *–Variety* [2M, 1W] ISBN: 0-8222-1676-0

★ **THE WEIR by Conor McPherson.** In a bar in rural Ireland, the local men swap spooky stories in an attempt to impress a young woman from Dublin who recently moved into a nearby "haunted" house. However, the tables are soon turned when she spins a yarn of her own. "You shed all sense of time at this beautiful and devious new play." *–The NY Times* "Sheer theatrical magic. I have rarely been so convinced that I have just seen a modern classic. Tremendous." *–The London Daily Telegraph* [4M, 1W] ISBN: 0-8222-1706-6

DRAMATISTS PLAY SERVICE, INC.
440 Park Avenue South, New York, NY 10016 212-683-8960 Fax 212-213-1539
postmaster@dramatists.com www.dramatists.com